ESSEN

CW00569650

CALIFORNIA

Original text by Richard Minnich
Updated by Richard Minnich

© Automobile Association Developments Limited 2008
First published 2008

ISBN 978-0-7495-5352-4

Published by AA Publishing, a trading name of Automobile Association Developments
Limited, whose registered office is Fanum House, Basing View, Basingstoke,
Hampshire RG21 4EA.
Registered number 1878835.

Colour separation: MRM Graphics Ltd
Printed and bound in Italy by Printer Trento S.r.l.

A03164
Maps in this title produced from
mapping © MAIRDUMONT / Falk Verlag 2007
Transport map © Communicarta Ltd, UK

About this book

Symbols are used to denote the following categories:

- ✚ map reference to maps on cover
- ✉ address or location
- ☎ telephone number
- ◷ opening times
- ✋ admission charge
- 🍴 restaurant or café on premises or nearby
- Ⓜ nearest underground train station
- 🚌 nearest bus/tram route
- 🚆 nearest overground train station
- ⛴ nearest ferry stop
- ✈ nearest airport
- ❓ other practical information
- 🛈 tourist information office
- ► indicates the page where you will find a fuller description

This book is divided into five sections.
The essence of California pages 6–19
Introduction; Features; Food and Drink; Short Break including the 10 Essentials

Planning pages 20–33
Before You Go; Getting There; Getting Around; Being There

Best places to see pages 34–55
The unmissable highlights of any visit to California

Best things to do pages 56–73
Good places to have lunch; best beaches; top activities; places to take the children and more

Exploring pages 74–185
The best places to visit in California, organized by area

💎 to 💎💎💎💎💎 denotes AAA rating

Maps

All map references are to the maps on the covers. For example, San Jose has the reference ✚ 4J – indicating the grid square in which it is to be found

Prices

An indication of the cost of restaurants and cafés at attractions is given by **$** signs: **$$$** denotes higher prices, **$$** denotes average prices, **$** denotes lower prices

Hotel prices

Prices are per room per night: **$** budget (under $100); **$$** moderate ($100–$250); **$$$** expensive (over $250)

Restaurant prices

Prices are for a three-course meal per person without drinks: **$** budget (under $15); **$$** moderate ($15–$30); **$$$** expensive (over $30)

Contents

BEST THINGS TO DO

EXPLORING...

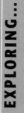

The essence of...

THE ESSENCE OF CALIFORNIA

One of the best things about California is that you rarely have to plan your vacation around the seasons. If you wish to relax on the beach, accommodations range from luxurious oceanside resorts to basic camping facilities. If you want continuous entertainment, the state abounds with theme parks, fairs and festivals.

For the explorer or seeker of beauty, the natural habitat is varied and unbeatable. For a tour of the coastline, the Amtrak rail system runs from the top to the bottom of the state and features plush, picture-windowed lounge cars. The landscape is perfect for the photographer.

features

California offers virtually every type of terrain, from desert to ocean to mountain, and environments ranging from small farming communities to giant metropolises that teem with cultural activity 24 hours a day.

If you're simply looking for rest and recuperation on your vacation, this is the place to visit. California is the epitome of "laid back," even in its busiest cities. At the same time the state is the nation's leader for fashion and fun.

So often when traveling, one's preconceived notion of a destination and the reality of that destination vary greatly. But whatever your most romantic visions of California might be, rest assured your visit to this kaleidoscopic state will not disappoint. It is almost impossible to overestimate the grandeur that awaits.

GEOGRAPHY
- Population: 36,200,000.
- Land area: 155,959sq miles (399,894sq km).
- Highest point: Mount Whitney (14,494ft/4,419m).
- Lowest point: Death Valley (282ft/86m below sea level).
- Capitol: Sacramento.

ECONOMIC FACTORS
● California is the leading agricultural economy in the US, primarily because of its fruit crops: prunes, oranges, grapes, peaches, apricots, figs, lemons, avocados, dates, nectarines and rice plums. Other agriculture products include cotton, walnuts, almonds, sugar beet, tomatoes, eggs, turkeys, sunflowers and honey.
● Napa (➤ 50–51) and Sonoma valleys (➤ 113, 114) are famous for their wineries.

SPORTS AND LEISURE
● Almost every conceivable sport, from boating and other watersports to sky-diving and rollerblading.

ANIMAL LIFE
● The Pacific Ocean is home to humpback whales, sea otters, seals, sea lions, dolphins, elephant seals, and blue whales, the largest mammals in the world, as well as hundreds of species of smaller fish. The pupfish (desert sardine) has even managed to survive in arid Death Valley (➤ 156).
● Land animals include bison, deer, Roosevelt elk, mountain goats, big-horn sheep, mountain lions, bobcats, wild burros and black bear.
● Desert creatures include iguanas, chuckawallas, pronghorn antelope, coyotes, kangaroo rats and various insects and reptiles, including the black widow spider and the rattlesnake.
● Birdlife ranges from the exotic white-faced ibis and the tiny hummingbird to the bald and golden eagle and the mundane sea gull.

PLANTS
● Unique trees in California are the eucalyptus, sequoias, redwoods, Joshua trees and many varieties of palm. Various cacti and flowers also abound year-round.

food & drink

Because of its immensely diverse cultural make-up, California is a food lover's paradise. The major cities have authentic cuisine from almost every nation in the world.

CUISINE

Nearby Mexico exerts a strong influence, especially encouraging the generous use of avocados and salsa. There are taquerias everywhere. Cilantro (coriander) is the spice of choice.

Sushi is fresh and popular. Chinese food, especially in San Francisco's Chinatown, is excellent. Fine dining establishments in the major cities feature delicious French cuisine.

All along the Coast are seafood houses to fit every budget. Fresh tuna and black cod are popular, while crab, oysters and jumbo shrimp cocktails satisfy lighter appetites.

North Beach in San Francisco has the best authentic Italian food, pasta can be found everywhere, Beverly Hills has great Jewish delis and Solvang (Central Coast) features fine Scandinavian food.

Most visitors to the area, however, look forward to sampling genuine California cuisine. Menus are renowned for catering to swimsuit figures by being light, healthy and diet-friendly. For vegetarians, there is a huge

year-round variety of locally grown vegetables (steamed), fresh salads with gourmet greens, and fresh fruits. Non-meat burgers and chicken are popular. The finest steaks can also be found, especially around the northern farming areas.

For a busy day of sightseeing, there are literally thousands of fast-food establishments. Even most of the small, inland towns have the major chains. In-N-Out Burger is a good choice for those on the run.

BEVERAGES

Health-conscious Californians consume more bottled water per capita than any other state in the US. This may be due to the fact

that a large part of the state has a desert-like climate and bottled water is easy to carry. Restaurants and markets offer a wide selection of both carbonated and uncarbonated types. Especially in the Palm Springs area, there are many roadside stands offering tasty "date shakes."

Although there are a few local breweries, imported beers seem to be favored by the locals, so you can find almost any of the popular brands. Mexico's Corona is a top choice. Micro-breweries are also popular, so check out some of the local beer-bistros for thirst-quenching treats.

The Mexican margarita is a time-tested standard. The martini is said to have originated in San Francisco and the Mai Tai cocktail was invented at Trader Vic's, at the original location in Oarkland.

Wine is said to appease and to have dietary and health considerations. Because so much excellent wine is produced in the state, the selection is overwhelming and costs are relatively affordable. Wineries of great renown include Mondavi, Beringer, Domaine Chandon, Louis M. Martini, Buena Vista, Sebastiani and Korbel Champagne. A

favorite is Mondavi's unfiltered Cabernet Sauvigon, while Pinot Noirs and Syrahs are also becoming increasingly popular. Along with the world-famous Napa Valley and Sonoma wines, the wineries of the central coastal area are gaining in prominence.

STAR GAZING

When dining and drinking in LA, remember that "star-gazing" may not necessarily be an exercise in astronomy. You could find yourself rubbing elbows with a celebrity straight off the screen as you satisfy your appetite. There is year-round patio dining, and casual attire is the norm. Most establishments accept all major credit cards.

short break

If you only have a short time to visit California and would like to take home some unforgettable memories, you can do something local and capture the real flavor of the area. The following suggestions will give you a wide range of sights and experiences that won't take long, won't cost very much and will make your visit very special.

● **Walk across the Golden Gate Bridge** (➤ 42) from San Francisco to Marin County. Spend an hour or so wandering around the small towns on the other side, then you can either walk or hop on a ferry back to San Francisco. Finish the day with a cable-car ride to view the city's marvelous architecture.

● **Spend a day hiking or backpacking** in one of the many national or state parks. The Joshua Tree National Monument is an especially good one (➤ 157).

● **Take a drive (or train)** along California's famous Route 1 for fantastic ocean views to the west and spectacular rolling hills or majestic mountain ranges to the east.

- **Visit a theme park**. Disneyland is the most well-known (➤ 40–41), but Balboa Park/San Diego Zoo is exciting too (➤ 36–37).

- **Go window-shopping** along Beverly Hills' exclusive Rodeo Drive (➤ 62) or El Paseo Drive in Palm Springs (➤ 62).

- **Take the one-day cruise** from San Pedro or Newport Beach to Catalina Island (➤ 38–39).

- **Take a drive through the Napa Valley** wine country, stopping at any of the wineries for a tour and some wine-tasting (➤ 50–51). This is also an excellent place to buy your souvenirs to take back home.

- **Spend the day** at one of the many beaches. Surf, sun or rent a bicycle, boogieboard or rollerblades.

- **Experience the excitement** of professional sports in San Francisco, San Diego or Los Angeles or attend a horse race at one of the major tracks.

● **Tour one of Hollywood's** motion picture studios
for an inside look at the making of screen magic.
Universal Studios (➤ 142) is the most famous.

Planning

Before you go

WHEN TO GO

JAN	FEB	MAR	APR	MAY	JUN	JUL	AUG	SEP	OCT	NOV	DEC
13°C	14°C	17°C	18°C	19°C	21°C	22°C	22°C	23°C	22°C	18°C	14°C
55°F	57°F	63°F	64°F	76°F	70°F	72°F	72°F	73°F	72°F	64°F	57°F

● High season   ● Low season

California is known for its diversity of climates. Generally speaking, the south is warmer and the north cooler. The bay areas are renowned for their fog. The mountainous areas are known for pleasant summers and snowy winters at the higher elevations.

The San Joaquin and Sacramento valleys are extremely hot during the summer months and cool and foggy the rest of the year. The rainy season is usually from November through April. As a rule, most parts of the state are cool in the evenings.

WHAT YOU NEED

● Required
○ Suggested
▲ Not required

Some countries require a passport to remain valid for a minimum period (usually at least six months) beyond the date of entry – check before you travel.

	UK	Germany	USA	Netherlands	Spain
Passport (or National Identity Card where applicable)	●	●	▲	●	●
Visa (regulations can change – check before you travel)	▲	▲	▲	▲	▲
Onward or Return Ticket	●	●	▲	●	●
Health Inoculations (tetanus and polio)	▲	▲	▲	▲	▲
Health Documentation (▶ 23, Health Insurance)	●	●	●	●	●
Travel Insurance	○	○	○	○	○
Driving License (national)	●	●	●	●	●
Car Insurance Certificate (if own vehicle)	○	○	○	○	○

WEBSITES

www.gocalifornia.ca.gov
www.visitcalifornia.com
www.onlyinsanfrancisco.com
www.touringca.com
www.disneyland.com

www.lawa.org/lax
www.flysfo.com
www.nps.gov/redw/
www.nps.gov/yose/

TOURIST OFFICES AT HOME

In the UK
Visit USA Association
☎ 09069 101020
(consumer line)
www.visitusa.org.uk

In the USA
California Division of Tourism
801 K Street, Suite 1600,
Sacramento, CA 95812
☎ 916/444-4429,
call-free 800/862-2543

HEALTH INSURANCE

There is no agreement for medical treatment between the US and other countries and all travelers MUST be covered by medical insurance (for an unlimited amount of medical costs is advisable). Treatment will be refused without evidence of insurance.

Medical insurance will cover you for dental treatment. In the event of any emergency, see your hotel concierge or consult the Yellow Pages for an emergency dentist.

TIME DIFFERENCES

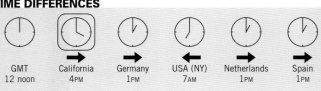

| GMT | California | Germany | USA (NY) | Netherlands | Spain |
| 12 noon | 4PM | 1PM | 7AM | 1PM | 1PM |

California is on Pacific Standard Time (PST); eight hours behind Greenwich Mean Time (GMT-8), but from early April, when clocks are put forward one hour, to late October, Daylight Saving Time (GMT-7) operates. California is also three hours behind the east coast of the USA (Eastern Standard Time/EST).

NATIONAL HOLIDAYS

Jan 1 *New Year's Day*
Jan (3rd Mon) *Martin Luther King Jr's Birthday*
Feb 12 *Lincoln's Birthday*
Feb (3rd Mon) *President's Day*

Jul 4 *Independence Day*
Sep (1st Mon) *Labor Day*
Oct (2nd Mon) *Columbus Day*
Nov 11 *Veteran's Day*

Nov (4th Thu) *Thanksgiving Day*
Dec 25 *Christmas Day*

On these days shops, banks and businesses close.

WHAT'S ON WHEN

The following are just a few of California's myriad festivals and celebrations.

January *Tournament of Roses Parade*, Pasadena
Palm Springs International Film Festival

February *Chinese New Year Celebration*, San Francisco
Napa Valley Mustard Celebration, Napa

March *International Asian Film Festival*, San Francisco
Los Angeles Marathon
Mendocino Whale Festival

April *Toyota Grand Prix*, Long Beach
Cherry Blossom Festival, San Francisco
Palm Desert Springfest, Palm Desert
Cinco De Mayo Celebration, state-wide

May *San Francisco International Film Fest*
Muscle Car Show, Bakersfield
Sacramento Jazz Jubilee
San Francisco Bay to Breakers, a race where people run in costume

June *Scottish Highlands Games and Gathering of the Clans*, Modesto
Amador County Wine Festival, Plymouth
Sonoma Valley Shakespeare Festival, Sonoma

July *Festival of Arts and Pageant of the Masters*, Laguna Beach
California Rodeo, Salinas
Greek Festival, Santa Barbara
San Francisco Marathon

August *Mozart Festival*, San Luis Obispo
Sawdust Festival, Laguna Beach
San Francisco Mime Troupe

Summer Park Season
Old Spanish Days Fiesta, Santa Barbara
Japanese Cultural Bazaar, Sacramento
California State Fair, Sacramento
Children's Festival of the Arts, Hollywood

September *Greek Food Festival*, Sacramento
Oktoberfest, Huntington Beach
Danish Days, Solvang
Monterey Jazz Festival, Monterey
Armenian Food Festival, San Francisco
Bowlful of Blues Festival, Ojai
California International Air Show, Salinas

October *Jazz Festival*, San Francisco
Rose Show, Santa Barbara
San Francisco Fleet week
Halloween, San Francisco

November *West Coast Ragtime Festival*, in various locations
Christmas Parade, Hollywood

December *America's Tallest Living Christmas Tree*, Ferndale
Newport Harbor Christmas Boat Parade, Newport Beach
Celebrity Cooks and Kitchens Tour, Mendocino
New Year's Eve Torchlight Parade, Big Bear Lake

Getting there

BY AIR

Los Angeles Airport

15 miles (24km) to city center

- 45–60 minutes
- 35 minutes
- 30 minutes

San Francisco Airport

16 miles (26km) to city center

- N/A
- 30–60 minutes
- 30 minutes

International direct flights operate into Los Angeles (LAX ☎ 310/646-5252) – one of the world's busiest airports – and San Francisco (SFO ☎ 650/821-8211). San Diego Airport (SAN) also has international flights but most stop en route first. Charter flights also use these airports. For the Federal Aviation Authority's air safety hotline tel: 800/322-7873.

BY CAR

Interstates 10, 15, 40 and 80 are the main routes into the state from the east. Interstate 5 is the principal route that runs from north to south. Route 101 is the smaller, more scenic route to drive while traveling along the coast. In some places it turns into Route 1. All gas stations have detailed maps.

BY RAIL AND BUS

There are Amtrak railroad stations in or near most of the major cities in California that connect from Las Vegas and other large places in the southwest. Many travelers find this a sensible way to see the state. Of particular interest is the scenic route that follows the coastline – the Coast Starlight – from Seattle to Los Angeles or on to San Diego via Oakland, Salinas, San Luis Obispo, Santa Barbara and the Malibu coast. For the most up-to-date information visit www.amtrak.com or call 800/872-7245).

For information about Greyhound Lines long-distance buses (tel: 800/231-2222; www.greyhound.com).

Getting around

PUBLIC TRANSPORTATION

Internal flights Flying is the quickest way of getting around California and is not all that expensive if you take advantage of deals offered by airlines. The international airports of San Francisco, Oakland, Los Angeles and San Diego connect with a number of regional airports.

Trains Rail service is provided by America's National Railroad Corporation, Amtrak. Carriages are clean, comfortable and rarely crowded. A Far Western Region Rail Pass (available only outside the US) gives 45 days unlimited travel over the far Western states.

Long-distance buses Buses are by far the cheapest way of getting around. Greyhound Lines operates an inter-city service and also links many smaller towns within California. The Ameripass (only available outside the US) gives 4, 5, 7, 15, 30 or 60 days' unlimited travel throughout the USA.

Ferries A ferry service links San Francisco with the Bay communities of Sausalito, Larkspur and Tiburon in scenic Marin County, and to Vallejo, Oakland and Alameda (departures from Pier 1, foot of Market Street). There is also a boat service from Long Beach and Newport Beach to Catalina Island.

Urban transportation Local communities and major cities are served by local bus services. In addition, San Francisco has cable-cars serving the downtown area and the BART train system covering the Bay areas. Los Angeles has its metrorail and San Diego has a trolley car service through the downtown area.

TAXIS

Cabs may be hailed on the street but few cruise outside tourist areas. If you are away from airports or major hotels it is best to phone for one (look under "cabs" in Yellow Pages). In most cities rates are high, except San Francisco because of its comparatively small size.

DRIVING

- Americans drive on the right.
- Seat belts must be worn in front seats at all times and in rear seats where fitted.
- Random breath-testing takes place. Never drive under the influence of alcohol.
- Fuel (gasoline or gas), leaded and unleaded, is sold in US gallons (3.8 liters). Most gas stations are self service. When removing the nozzle from the pump you must lift or turn the lever to activate it. Fuel is more expensive in remote areas and you may be charged more if paying by credit card.
- If you break down in a rented car, phone the emergency number on the dashboard. Summon help from emergency telephones located along freeways (every half mile) and remote highways (every 2 miles/3.2km), or sit tight and wait for the cruising highway patrol or state patrol to spot you (a raised bonnet should help).
- Speed limits are as follows:
  On rural interstate roads (motorways) 55–70mph (88–113kph)
  On many freeways (two-lane or more carriageways) 65mph (105kph)
  In residential and business districts and school zones 25mph (40kph)
  or as signposted

CAR RENTAL

If you are planning to rent a car, consider taking advantage of one of the fly/drive programs many airlines offer before you go. Otherwise most car rental companies have offices throughout the state. Charges depend on the size of car, locale and time of year. Pay by credit card to avoid a hefty cash deposit.

None of the major companies will rent to anyone under the age of 25. It may be possible to find a local company that will do so, but be prepared to pay a loaded insurance premium.

It is advisable to find out whether your own insurance would cover damage to a rented car, and what the details are of Collision Damage Waiver (CDW).

FARES AND CONCESSIONS

Students Upon production of ID proving student status, there are discounts available on travel, theater and museum tickets, plus at some nightspots. It is always worth asking at the outset.

Senior citizens For anyone over the age of 62 there is a tremendous variety of discounts on offer (upon proof of age). Both Amtrak (train) and Greyhound (bus), as well as many US airlines, offer (smallish) percentage reductions on fares. Museums, art galleries, attractions, cinemas, and even hotels offer small discounts, and as the definition of senior can drop to as low as 55, it is always worth enquiring.

Being there

TOURIST OFFICES

Anaheim/Orange County Visitor & Convention Bureau, 800 West Katella Avenue, Anaheim, CA 92802
☎ 714/765-8857

California Deserts Tourism Association, 37–115 Palm View Road, Rancho Mirage, CA 92270
☎ 760/328-9256

Los Angeles Convention &Visitors Bureau, 685 Figueroa Street, Los Angeles, CA 90017
☎ 213/689-8822

Monterey Peninsula Visitors & Convention Bureau, 150 Oliver Street, PO Box 1770, Monterey, CA 93940
☎ 831/649-1770

Palm Springs Tourism, 777 N Canyon Drive, Suite 201, Palm Springs, CA 92264
☎ 760/778-8415

Sacramento Convention & Visitors Bureau, 1608 I Street, Sacramento, CA 95814
☎ 916/264-7777

San Diego Convention & Visitors Bureau, 401 B Street, Suite 1400, San Diego, CA 92101
☎ 619/236-1212

San Francisco Convention & Visitors Bureau, 201 Third Street, Suite 900, San Francisco, CA 94103
☎ 415/974-6900

MONEY

The American monetary unit is the dollar ($), which is divided into 100 cents. There are coins of 1 cent (penny), 5 cents (nickel), 10 cents (dime), 25 cents (quarter), 50 cents (half dollar) and 1 dollar. Bills (notes) are available in denominations of 1, 2 (rarely seen), 5, 10, 20, 50 and 100 dollars.

POSTAL SERVICES

Post offices are plentiful in cities. Stamps are also sold from stamp machines in hotels and shops but have a 25 percent mark up. Main post offices in larger cities normally open 8–6 (noon Sat); closed Sun.
☎ 213/483-3745 (Los Angeles); ☎ 415/487-8981 (San Francisco).

TIPS/GRATUITIES

Yes ✓ No ✗		
Restaurants	✓	15–20%
Cafeterias/fast-food outlets	✗	
Bars	✓	15–20%
Cabs	✓	15–20%
Porters	✓	$1 per bag
Chambermaids	✓	$1 per day
Toilet attendants	✗	

TELEPHONES

Telephones are located in hotel and motel lobbies, drugstores, restaurants, garages and in roadside kiosks. Exact change in 5, 10 and 25 cent pieces is required to place a call. For internal calls dial 1 before the number when the area code is different from the one on the phone you are using. For the operator dial 0, for directory assistance dial 411.

International Dialling Codes
From the USA to:
UK: 011 44
Germany: 011 49
Netherlands: 011 31
Spain: 011 34

Emergency telephone numbers
Police 911
Fire 911
Ambulance 911

EMBASSIES AND CONSULATES

UK ☎ 310/481-0031 (LA)
Germany ☎ 323/930-2703 (LA),
☎ 415/775-1061 (SF)

Netherlands ☎ 310/268-1598 (LA)
Spain ☎ 323/938-0158 (LA),
☎ 415/922-2995 (SF)

HEALTH ADVICE

Sun advice California enjoys a lot of sunshine with more than 250 clear days a year. Along the coast mornings can be hazily overcast and sea breezes (especially in the north) can make it feel cooler than it is. Protect the skin at all times.

Drugs Quick-remedy medicines such as aspirin are readily available at any pharmacy (drugstore). For tablets containing acetaminophen read paracetamol. Also, many pain-killing pills available "over the counter" at home may need a prescription in the US.

Safe water It is quite safe to drink tap water. In hotels and restaurants a nice touch is that water, generally ice cold, is provided free with meals. Bottled water is also widely available but is not as popular as in Europe.

PERSONAL SAFETY

California is certainly not crime free and drugs are a problem, but exercise due caution, especially in downtown areas, and you should be safe. Away from these areas crime is quite low key. Some precautions:
● If confronted by a mugger, hand over your money.
● If driving do not stop the car in any unlit or deserted urban area.
Police assistance: ☎ 911 from any call box

ELECTRICITY

The power supply is 110–115 volts. Round 3-hole sockets taking plugs with 2 flat pins in a parallel position, with an upper, round, earth pin for earthed appliances. European visitors should bring a voltage transformer as well as an adaptor.

OPENING HOURS

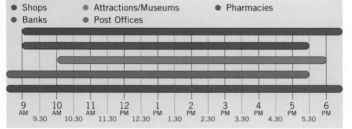

In addition to the times shown above, many shops, particularly department stores within shopping malls, are open evenings and during afternoons on Sunday. Some supermarkets and grocery shops open 24 hours. Banks open until 5:30pm Friday and some major banks open on Saturday. Banks in some major towns and tourist areas may have longer hours. Some pharmacies open from 7am to 9pm or even midnight, while some open 24 hours. Opening times of attractions and museums vary (see individual entries in the What to See section). Some post offices open Saturday 8am–1pm.

LANGUAGE

English is the official language of the USA. Californians, however, are a fascinating mix of cultures, most notably of Spanish or Mexican extraction. In fact, Spanish is heard throughout California. The five largest cities in California: Los Angeles, San Diego, San Francisco, San Jose and Sacramento bear Spanish names. However, although English is the native language there are many differences between its British and American usage. Some of the more commonly encountered are listed below:

holiday	*vacation*	lift	*elevator*
fortnight	*two weeks*	eiderdown	*comforter*
ground floor	*first floor*	hotel porter	*bellhop*
first floor	*second floor*	chambermaid	*room maid*
flat	*apartment*	surname	*last name*
cheque	*check*	25 cent coin	*quarter*
traveller's cheque	*traveler's check*	banknote	*bill*
1 cent coin	*penny*	banknote (colloquial)	*greenback*
5 cent coin	*nickel*	dollar (colloquial)	*buck*
10 cent coin	*dime*	cashpoint	*automatic teller*
aubergine	*eggplant*	confectionery	*candy*
chips (potato)	*fries*	prawns	*shrimp*
crisps (potato)	*chips*	soft drink	*soda*
courgette	*zucchini*	spirit	*liquor*
car	*automobile*	motorway	*freeway*
bonnet (of car)	*hood*	main road	*highway*
boot (of car)	*trunk*	petrol	*gas*
caravan	*trailer*	tram	*streetcar*
lorry	*truck*	underground	*subway*
shop	*store*	trousers	*pants*
chemist (shop)	*drugstore*	nappy	*diaper*
cinema	*movie theater*	glasses	*eyeglasses*
pavement	*sidewalk*	post	*mail*
toilet	*lavatory*	post code	*zip code*

Best places to see

1

Balboa Park

This immense expanse of parks and museums includes the world-renowned San Diego Zoo.

A 100-tone chime serenades from the 200ft (61m) California Tower, creating an exquisite backdrop for the historical buildings, museums and gardens of this 1,200-acre (486ha) park. Start your visit from the main thoroughfare, El Prado (The Promenade). Here you'll find original exhibit halls from the 1915 Panama–California International Exposition, most notably the Casa del Prado. The Timken Museum of Art, a few blocks south, has interesting Russian icons among its exhibits.

At the park's center are several small museums: San Diego History Museum, Museum of Photographic

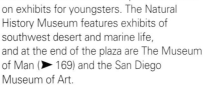

Arts, Model Railroad Museum and Hall of Champions (sports). The nearby Reuben H. Fleet Space Theater and Science Center provides hands-on exhibits for youngsters. The Natural History Museum features exhibits of southwest desert and marine life, and at the end of the plaza are The Museum of Man (➤ 169) and the San Diego Museum of Art.

Visit any of the three stages of the Globe Theatre to see contemporary or Shakespearean plays, or enjoy a summer musical at The Starlight Bowl.

Simply stated, the **San Diego Zoo** is among the finest zoos in the world. The 100 acres (40ha) simulate the natural habitats of the 800 species living here, and allows expansive roaming of its 4,000 animals, which include the only pair of pandas in the US. The Children's Zoo offers close-up views. There are guided bus tours, as well as an aerial tramway that rises 170ft (52m) over the zoo's grottoes and mesas, providing a fine overview of the park.

🚼 11Z ✉ 1 mile (1.61km) north of downtown San Diego ☎ 619/239-0512 🕐 Daily 9–4:30 (4 in winter) ✋ Moderate 🍴 Restaurants, stands ($$) 🚌 7, 7A or 7B from downtown ❓ Visitor Center sells multi-day passports to the park; free in-park tram

San Diego Zoo

☎ 619/234-3153; www.sandiegozoo.com 🕐 Daily 9–4; zoo grounds close at 6pm ✋ Inexpensive

2 Catalina Island

**Known as "The Island of Romance,"
Catalina Island is a perfect blend of
relaxed resort, pristine shoreline and
untouched wilderness.**

Discovered in 1542 by Juan Rodriguez Cabrillo,
Santa Catalina (commonly called Catalina Island) is

roughly 26 miles (42km) from the mainland. One of the eight California Channel Islands, it is 21 miles (34km) long and 8 miles (13km) wide. No cars are allowed on the island, so use the public transportation or rent the electric golf carts and bicycles available.

In 1811, the indigenous Gabrileño Indians were forced to resettle on the mainland, leaving the island that later became the private property of the Wrigley family, the chewing gum heirs. Today, 86 percent of the island is owned by the non-profit Santa Catalina Island Conservancy, established in 1972 to preserve the island's natural beauty. The island provides a welcome retreat from mainland crowds, with its silent beaches, water sports, picturesque pier and deep-sea fishing.

The 1929 Avalon Casino is the most famous building on the island, best known for its art deco ballroom, which in its heyday was host to many of the world's most famous orchestras and big bands. The Catalina Island Museum, on the first floor of the Casino, exhibits the island's history. The Wrigley Mansion, with its botanical gardens, and the Avalon Pier, in the middle of Avalon Bay, provide fine views of the interior hills and the breathtaking shoreline.

✚ 9Y 🖂 Visitors Center, Green Pier ☎ 310/510-1520; www.catalina.com ◷ Daily 8–5 ✋ Travel moderate; exhibits inexpensive 🍴 Restaurants ($$$) ⛴ Catalina Express 310/519-1212 or 800/618-5533; 1 hour each way; hourly from San Pedro or Long Beach.Catalina Passenger Service 949/673-5245; 75 mins each way; departs from Balboa Pavilion 9, returns 4:30 ✖ Helicopter Service from Island Express 800/228-2566; 15 mins each way

3 Disneyland® Park

www.disneyland.com

Disneyland Park sets the standard for theme parks. This "happiest place on earth" attracts around 12 million visitors each year.

Children and adults alike are enchanted by the illusion and entertainment of "magic kingdom," opened in 1955. The 80-acre (32ha) park is divided into eight sections, offering such diverse attractions as fantasy rides, musical performances, parades, restaurants and shops.

A series of pastel-colored walkways lead from the central plaza at the end of Main Street, U.S.A. into the various themed areas, each with their own attractions. Mickey's Toontown brings out the kid in everyone; Adventureland offers a jungle boat ride and the charming "Tiki Room." New Orleans Square has a Mississippi steamwheeler, the "Pirates of the Caribbean" attraction and the "Haunted Mansion."

In Frontierland, you can career down Big Thunder Mountain Railroad on a runaway train or raft across to Tom Sawyer Island. Critter Country is the home of the "Splash Mountain" flume ride. Fantasyland begins when you cross the moat to Sleeping Beauty Castle, while Tomorrowland explores the future with attractions like "Space Mountain" and "Star Tours." For the courageous, the "Indiana Jones Adventure" takes you on a trek to the Temple of the Forbidden Eye. Disney characters roam the streets and pose for pictures. Disney's California Adventure Park, a celebration of the State's past and future, is next to Disneyland.

🚊 10X ✉ 1313 Harbor Boulevard, Anaheim ☎ 714/781-4565 🕓 Summer Mon–Fri 9am–midnight (until 1am Sat; winter Mon–Fri 10–6 (until 9pm weekends, public hols). Hours can vary, check first ✋ Expensive ❓ Hours and prices subject to change; on busy days park at the Disneyland Hotel and ride the monorail to the park

4 Golden Gate Bridge and National Recreation Area

The Golden Gate Bridge is quite easily the most beautiful and easily recognized bridge in the world.

The rust-colored symbol of the West Coast stands as a beacon at the entrance of San Francisco Bay. Built in 1937 it is beautiful and impressive from any angle. Often cloaked in fog, the bridge is extraordinarily graceful and delicate in design even though its overall length is 8,981ft (2,737m), and the stolid towers reach 746ft (227m) high. Connecting San Francisco to Marin County and northern California, the suspension bridge withstands winds of up to 100mph (161kph) and swings as much as 27ft (8m). Enjoy the drive over, or walk across for a truly spectacular perspective.

Golden Gate Park, the largest urban national park in the US, covers 74,000 acres (29,959ha) from San Mateo County to Tomales Bay. The giant recreation area offers many attractions, including Fort Mason on San Francisco's waterfront. A former military embarkation point for soldiers during World War II, today the fort is the site of museums, theaters, galleries, restaurants and the last unaltered, operational liberty ship, the SS *Jeremiah O'Brien*.

The Golden Gate Promenade is a scenic bayshore hike stretching 3.5 miles (5.5km) from Hyde Street Pier to Fort Point and beyond, across the Golden Gate Bridge. Among other sights in this impressive area are The Presidio, Baker Beach, Cliff House, Ocean Beach and Fort Funston, most of which are accessible by San Francisco's MUNI system.

🚼 3H

Golden Gate Bridge ☎ MUNI 28; 415/554-6999 (hotline)

✋ Free northbound; southbound toll inexpensive

❓ Alcatraz tour info 415/981-7625

Recreation Area

✉ GGNRA, Building 201, Fort Mason, San Francisco

☎ 415/561-4700 (information line) 🕐 Mon–Fri 9:30–4:30

✋ Moderate 🍴 Cafés, stands ($)

5 Hearst Castle

www.hearstcastle.com

William Randolph Hearst's tribute to excess and grandiosity crowns a hillside above the village of San Simeon.

The history of this fabulous castle dates back to 1865, when George Hearst purchased 40,000 acres

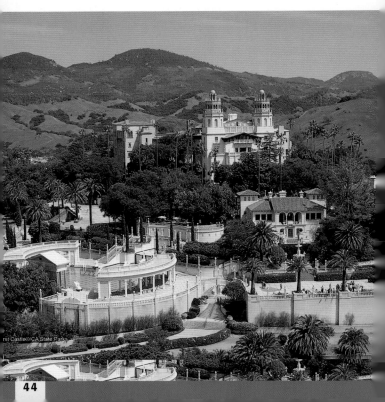

rst Castle©CA State Parks

(16,194ha) of Mexican land adjacent to San Simeon Bay. His son, newspaper magnate William Randolph Hearst, began the castle when he took possession of the land in 1919, which now numbers 250,000 acres

(101,215ha). Steamers and chain-driven trucks were used to transport materials to the remote spot, but the palatial residence was not completed until 1947.

Casa Grande, as the mammoth mansion is called, boasts more than 100 rooms filled with priceless objects of art and antiques. It was donated to the California Park Service in 1957.

Among the mansion's exquisite attributes are Gothic fireplaces, Flemish tapestries, Renaissance paintings and ceilings ranging in style from 16th-century Spanish to 18th-century Italian. In its prime, the doge's suite was reserved for the most important guests: presidents, visiting heads of state such as Winston Churchill and Hollywood luminaries. Marble colonnades and statuary flanking the indoor and outdoor pools replicate figures of antiquity.

There are also five greenhouses with over 700,000 annuals providing year-round color, tennis courts and a movie theater (in which Walt Disney hosted the first screening of *Snow White* in 1938). There are also two libraries, riding stables and the world's largest private zoo.

✚ 5L ✉ 750 Hearst Castle Road, San Simeon ☎ 805/927-2020 or 800/444-4445
🕓 Daily 8:20–3:20 (Dec start times may vary). Five different tours offered daily
✋ Moderate ❓ 214 miles (345km) southeast of San Francisco; 242 miles (390km) northwest of Los Angeles; parking just off Hwy 1 with shuttles buses to the castle. Four tours, priced separately. Tour 1 is recommended for first-time visitors. Reservations suggested

6 Hollywood

A one-time cow town, Hollywood is now the movie-making capital of the world and trend-setting center of glamour, glitter and excess.

Hollywood Boulevard is a relatively short street, but is one of the best known of all Los Angeles thoroughfares. Its wealth of art deco architecture has elevated it to the status of national historic district. From the 1920s to the 1950s, Hollywood boasted some of the country's largest movie palaces and exclusive department stores. As the movie industry expanded outward, Hollywood lost its luster, but the faded star is now staging a comeback.

The Hollywood Roosevelt Hotel (➤ 144), site of the first Academy Awards, has been renovated and displays historical film memorabilia throughout. An ambitious three-block redevelopment project around Sid Grauman's

1927 Chinese Theatre (now Mann's Chinese Theatre; ➤ 140–141) offers shops, restaurants, movie theaters and the Hollywood Studio Museum.

Hollywood abounds with guided bus tours of every sort. Walking tours of its bronze-starred Walk of Fame are extremely popular. Begun in 1960 with only eight stars, there are now close to 3,000 celebrity handprints. The 1920s Hollywood sign can best be viewed by venturing up Beachwood Canyon on the eastern edge of Hollywood or from Griffith Observatory, high atop Mount Hollywood.

Paramount Studio provides a peek into the world of film-making. Free tickets to several popular TV shows are readily available outside Mann's Theatre or through the major network studios.

Hawkers along Sunset and Hollywood boulevards offer surprisingly accurate maps to celebrity homes at a low price; you can drive yourself or take a bus tour.

✚ 9W ✉ Hollywood Visitors Bureau, 333 South Hope Street ☎ 213/624-7300; 323/937-3661 (LA TOURS); 323/469-8311 (Hollywood Chamber of Commerce)
🍴 Numerous restaurants, some open 24 hours ($–$$$)

7 Monterey Peninsula

"This is the California men dreamed of years ago. The face of the earth as the Creator intended it to look." Henry Miller

For more than 300 years the Monterey Peninsula has enchanted everyone who has seen it. Formed by the Monterey and Carmel bays, the peninsula juts into the Pacific Ocean 120 miles (194km) south of San Francisco. Pristine beaches, craggy rock formations and wind- and wave-warped cypresses make the area among the most popular scenic spots in the world.

Nowhere in California is the state's Latin heritage more prevalent than in Monterey, where its exquisitely restored adobe buildings give testimony to the Spanish and Mexican periods of California history.

From art galleries in Carmel (➤ 122) to the grand estates in the dense woods of the Del Monte

Forest, the scenic 17-Mile Drive through the forest between Pacific Grove and Carmel is almost incomparable in beauty.

The legacy of famed California author John Steinbeck can be traced at The National Steinbeck Center in Salinas (➤ 124; open daily). You can also visit his preserved cottage in nearby Pacific Grove.

Carmel-by-the-Sea is an enchanting seaside village. Much of its architecture is reminiscent of rural European and early California styles.

Monterey's touristy Fisherman's Wharf has a magnificent promenade of fish markets, seafood restaurants, shops and theaters. For a different perspective, a sail can be arranged aboard the restored tall ship *Californian*.

Established at the turn of the 20th century by a group of writers and artists, Carmel was originally a planned resort. As its popularity soared, it took on the reputation of something completely different: an exclusive bohemian retreat. Resisting efforts for modernization, Carmel has preserved its idyllic setting. At Point Lobos State Reserve, 2 miles (3.5km) south of Carmel, harbor seals, gray whales and California sea lions frolic among a variety of sea birds and pelicans, a sight seen nowhere else in the world.

🚻 4K ✉ 122 miles (197km) southeast of San Francisco; 334 miles (539km) northwest of LA ☎ 831/649-1770 (Visitors Bureau); 831/649-7118 (State Historical Park); 831/624-2522 (Carmel Business Association); 831/659-0333 (Steinbeck Country Tours) 🍴 Various restaurants ($–$$$) 🚌 Monterey–Salinas Transit

8 Napa Valley

Only 30 miles (48km) long and 3 miles (5km) across at its widest, this little valley boasts some 220 wineries.

Leader of the American wine industry, the Napa Valley boasts such well-known names as Robert Mondavi, Domaine Chandon, Beringer and Sterling. Although the greatest concentration of wineries is along State Route 29, north from Napa to Calistoga, knowledgeable travelers use the Silverado Trail, a scenic, vineyard-lined parallel road along the eastern edge of the valley.

The city of Napa is the largest, although each of the valley towns has its charms. In Calistoga there are spas and geysers, one of which shoots 60ft (18m) into the air every 40 minutes. St. Helena claims many of the region's best dining and lodging choices, as well as a wine library and the Silverado Museum. An ancient volcanic eruption from Washington's Mount St. Helens around 3 million years ago caused the giant redwoods of California to become instantly petrified. You'll find the Petrified Forest between Calistoga and Santa Rosa.

Outside of these towns lie more wineries, markets, inns, quiet picnic areas and historic parklands. Most visitors tour the vineyards, which offer a look at the wine-making process and feature wine-tastings, but there are also five different walking tours of the incredible architectural highlights of the valley (maps available at the information center). If possible, avoid the crowded summer weekends. Most vintners now charge a small fee for the tastings and a few require reservations.

🚌 4G ✉ Visitor Information Center, 1310 Napa Town Center, Napa ☎ 707/226-7459 (Visitor Information Center), 707/253-2111; www.napavalley.com/visitorsinfo; 800/427-4124 (Napa Valley Wine Train) 🕐 Hours vary; some tours require reservations 👋 Free–inexpensive 🍴 Restaurants in the towns ($$–$$$)

9 Redwood National Park

www.nps.gov/redw/

A vast forest of giant redwoods grows naturally nowhere else in the country except in this coastal region.

Before California's famous gold rush, and the resulting surge of new population, the world's tallest trees blanketed an area 30 miles (48km) wide and 450 miles (726km) long. The majority of today's redwood "stands" are along US 101, from Leggett north to Crescent City. It is about a five-hour drive from San Francisco to the southern edge of the Redwood Forest, via the scenic coastal highway.

A small segment of old growth redwoods and outstanding coastal scenery have been protected in the 106,000-acre (42,915ha) Redwood National Park. Eight miles (13km) of shoreline roads and more than 150 miles (242km) of trails afford close-up encounters with these trees and the abundant plant and animal life they nurture.

The three main state parks within the Park's boundaries are Prairie Creek, Del Norte Coast and Jedediah Smith. Campers favor Prairie Creek

because of its herds of native Roosevelt elk and expansive beach (Gold Bluffs Beach). Lady Bird Johnson Cove is especially beautiful. Don't miss the Libby Tree, the tallest known tree, which towers to over 368ft (112m).

A drive through Del Norte Coast park allows you to enjoy spectacular ocean views and the inland forest simultaneously. The giant redwoods grow closest to the shoreline at the Damnation Creek Trail. In the spring, this area is the best place to view the abundant growth of rhododendrons and azaleas.

At the north end of the park, the Jedediah Smith terrain gives you an elevated perspective.

➕ 2B ✉ National Park Headquarters, 1111 Second Street, Crescent City ☎ 707/464-6101 (Redwood National Park Information Center) ✋ Moderate 🍴 Restaurants ($); picnic facilities

10 Yosemite National Park

www.nps.gov/yose/

By any standards, Yosemite is the most spectacular national park in the country. To call it awe-inspiring would be an understatement.

Nearly 70 percent of the annual visitors to Yosemite National Park arrive in the summer and stay within the compact but awesome Yosemite Valley. The main section of the park, just 7sq miles (18sq km) in area, boasts monumental granite walls and high-diving waterfalls, but there remains almost 1,200sq miles (3,076sq km) of splendor to explore. Beyond are such natural wonders as giant sequoias, alpine meadows, lakes and trout-filled streams, Glacier Point and majestic 13,000ft (3,963m) Sierra Nevada peaks. Giant sequoias are located in the Mariposa

Grove, near the park's south entrance, about 30 miles (48km) from Yosemite Valley. In this great forest, over 200 trees measure more than 10ft (3m) in diameter.

Some of the park's finest scenery is in the wild back country along the Tioga Road. There are rustic lodges and campgrounds (permit camping). In the main valley, 3,500ft (1,067m) El Capitan attracts climbers from around the world.

Off-season visits are also spectacular. In fall, leaves turn from green to crimson and gold and

nights are cool and pleasant. Spring offers
magnificent waterfalls that create rainbows across
the valley floor. For the ambitious, there's the 200-
mile (322km) John Muir Trail that follows the
naturalist's path through the wilderness. For many,
the winter provides solitude and restores the raw
grandeur of the park. The ski season at Badger Pass
lasts from the end of November until mid-April.

➕ 8Q ✉ Yosemite Valley Visitors Center ☎ 209/
372-0200 ⏰ Apr–May daily 9–6; Jul–Aug daily 8–8;
Sep–Oct daily 8–6; Nov–Mar daily 9–5 ✋ Moderate
🍴 Restaurants ($)

Best things to do

Good places to have lunch

Clementine ($)
Breakfast/lunch café near Century City.
✉ 1751 Ensley Avenue, Los Angeles ☎ 310/552-1080

Dottie's True Blue Café ($)
Great diner for typical American food. Breakfast and lunch.
✉ 522 Jones Street, San Francisco ☎ 415/885-2767

Fat City Café and Bar ($–$$))
Art nouveau, old European atmosphere with stained glass and a 100-year-old bar. Light entrées and rich desserts.
✉ 1001 Front Street, Sacramento ☎ 916/446-6769

Gabriella Café ($$)

Californian/Italian cuisine.

✉ 910 Cedar Street, Santa Cruz ☎ 831/457-1677

Gladstones 4 Fish ($$)

Fresh seafood on the beach.

✉ 17300 Pacific Coast Highway, Pacific Palisade, Los Angeles ☎ 310/GL4-FISH, 310/454-3474

Karl Strauss' Old Columbia Brewery & Grill ($$)

Specialties are burgers, fresh fish and German-style sausage. Watch the microbrewery process while you sip a cold one.

✉ 1157 Columbia Street, San Diego ☎ 619/234-2739

Pier 23 Café ($$)

✉ The Embarcadero (Pier 23) at Broadway, San Francisco ☎ 415/362-5125

Pinks Hot Dog Stand ($)

Grunge stand with limo parking and great dogs and burgers.

✉ Highland and Melrose, Los Angeles

Tarpy's Roadhouse ($$)

Steak, seafood and American comfort food; extensive wine list.

✉ 2999 Monterey-Salinas Highway, Monterey ☎ 831/647-1444

The Tea Pavilion ($$)

Great views in Balboa Park accompanied by sushi, miso soup, Japanese noodles and specialty teas.

✉ Balboa Park, San Diego ☎ 619/231-0048

Unusual annual events

February
National Date Festival and Fair (camel and ostrich races), Indio
☎ 760/863-8247.

March
Snowfest (West's largest), Tahoe City ☎ 530/546-5253.

Mendocino/Fort Bragg Whale Festival ☎ 707/961-6300.

May
Frog Jumping Contest, Angel's Camp ☎ 209/736-2561.

Dixieland Jazz Jubilee, Sacramento ☎ 916/372-5277.

Great Monterey Squid Festival, Monterey ☎ 831/649-6544.

July
Gilroy Garlic Festival, Gilroy ☎ 408/842-1625.

October
Grand National Rodeo, Horse, and Stock Show, Daly City (world-class) ☎ 415/404-4100.

November
Doo Dah Parade (spoof of famous Rose Parade), Pasadena
☎ 626/440-7379.

Monarch butterfly migration to Pismo Beach's Butterfly Trees, November to March.

Best shopping areas

LOS ANGELES
Melrose Avenue
Three-mile (5km) strip of shops, from Aardvark's used clothing to vintage stores and upscale boutiques.
✉ Between Highland and Doheny, Hollywood

Rodeo Drive
Renowned as being the most exclusive and expensive shopping area on the West Coast. Top designer clothes and accessories.
✉ Between Santa Monica and Wilshire boulevards, Beverly Hills

MONTEREY
Cannery Row
Unique shops and restaurants line this nautical area, made famous by John Steinbeck's novel *Cannery Row*.
✉ Fisherman's Wharf

ORANGE COUNTY
South Coast Plaza
This is Orange County's largest and most exclusive mall, with three huge sections connected by free tram. All major department stores are located within this complex, along with a wide variety of specialty stores.

PALM SPRINGS
El Paseo
Exclusive shops that rival Beverly Hills' Rodeo Drive. Art galleries.
✉ Visitors Center, 2901 N Palm Canyon Drive
☎ 760/778-8418

SAN DIEGO
Fashion Valley Mall
This and Mission Valley are the city's two main shopping centres. Six major department stores.

✉ 352 Fashion Valley Road

Gaslamp Quarter
A must for the arts and crafts crowd. The Quarter takes in 38 acres (15ha) in the National Historic District.

✉ Fifth Avenue from Broadway to the waterfront

Old Town
Small gift boutiques and cafés among flower gardens, fountains and courtyards in the style of a Mexican marketplace. One of the best antiques shopping areas in Southern California. Bargain prices for valuable items at local antiques shops.

✉ Mason Street and San Diego Avenue

SAN FRANCISCO
Chinatown
Asian specialty shops, fresh produce, and incredible architecture (➤ 84–85).

✉ Bordered by Broadway, Bush, Kearny and Powell streets

Fisherman's Wharf
Street performers entertain as you explore the 100 shops and restaurants clustered around the piers (➤ 83).

✉ Between The Embarcadero and Columbus Avenue

Movie locations

Alcatraz Island, San Francisco – *The Birdman of Alcatraz* (1962);
Escape From Alcatraz (1979); *The Rock* (1996)

D Street, Petaluma – *American Graffiti* (1973)

Golden Gate Bridge, San Francisco – *A View to A Kill* (1985)

Muir Woods, Marin County – *Vertigo* (1958)

Musso and Frank Grill, 6667 Hollywood Boulevard, Hollywood –
Ed Wood (1994); *Ocean's 11* (2001)

Regent Beverly Wilshire Hotel, Wilshire Boulevard, Los Angeles
– *Beverly Hills Cop* (1984); *Pretty Woman* (1990)

Union Station, Figueroa Street, downtown Los Angeles – *The
Way We Were* (1973); *Blade Runner* (1982); *Bugsy* (1991)

Van Nuys Airport, 16461 Sherman Way, Van Nuys, San Fernando
Valley – *Casablanca* (1942)

Venice High School, 1300 Venice Boulevard, Venice – *Grease*
(1978)

7121 Lonzo Street, Tujunga – *E.T. the Extra Terrestrial* (1982)

Best beaches

East Beach The most centrally located of Santa Barbara's beaches, with lots of activities

La Jolla Small, private beaches set inbetween cliffs

Laguna Beach Quaint, artistic community at the mid-point between LA and San Diego. Spacious beaches and coves, ideal for watching sea lions

Newport–Huntington beaches Orange County's largest and most popular beach areas. Lots of boating opportunities. Huntington is also known for its international surfing and volleyball tournaments

Ocean Beach Less crowded San Diego beach with great shops and restaurants

Pacific Beach Known to the locals as "PB." A large area with shopping and restaurants; also close to San Diego's attractions

Santa Cruz Beach California's only beach area with an amusement park on its boardwalk. Roller-coasters, bumper cars, haunted castles, Ferris wheel

Santa Monica Beach Large accessible beach for those visiting LA and Hollywood. Long cycle path connects to Venice Beach to the south

Stinson Beach North of San Francisco, with state park access and hiking trails. Cold in winter; perfect in summer

Zuma Beach At the north end of Malibu. Excellent for surfing, volleyball and whale-watching during winter

Places to take the children

Along with attractions already featured in the book, the following are ideal for children.

Atascadero Lake Park and Charles Paddock Zoo

Intimate zoo with jaguars from Brazil, Bengal tigers, pink flamingos and lots of chimps. Nominal entry fee. Next to the zoo is a beautiful lake with picnic facilities.

✉ State Route 41, south of Paso Robles ☎ 805/461-5080; www.atascadero.org ⏰ Zoo: daily 10–4, 10–5 in summer. Lake Park: daily until sundown

Kidseum

Kids won't even realize they're being educated about world cultures as they take part in the story-telling, puppet shows and other exhibits at this interactive museum.

✉ 1802 Main Street, Santa Ana ☎ 714/567-3600 (Bowers Museum and College of Art); www.bowers.org/kidseum ⏰ Summer: Tue–Sun noon–4; winter: Sat–Sun 11–4

Lake Nacimiento Resort

Great outdoor activities, including fishing and diving. Features a full-service marina and dock where you can rent anything from paddle boats to jet-skis to pontoon boats. Lodge, camp-grounds and RV facilities.

✉ County Road G–14 out of Paso Robles ☎ 805/238-3256; www.nacimientoresort.com ⏰ Daily to sundown

Legoland California

This Danish import opened in 1999, and the entire park is built out of lego pieces. Over 50 rides, exhibits and shows to choose from. Usually very packed.

✉ 1 Lego Drive, Carlsbad ☎ 760/918-5346; www.legoland.com/california ⏰ Call for hours ✋ Expensive

Paramount's Great America

The Bay area's place for roller coasters and other daredevil rides. Fort-Fun is an interactive parent/child area. Top Gun and Smurf Woods rides are the most popular. Also features stage shows, musicals, puppet shows and wildlife shows.

✉ Great American Parkway, Santa Clara, south of San Francisco ☎ 408/988-1776; www.pgathrills.com 🕓 Sat–Sun 10–7; weekdays summer only

Raging Waters

The Bay area's only water theme park, with large and long waterslides designed to please. There are over 30 different attractions. Older children will love the innertube rides.

✉ Lake Cunningham Park, 2333 S White Road, San Jose ☎ 408/238-9900; www.rwsplash.com 🕓 May–Sep, call for hours

Six Flags Magic Mountain

Specializing in thrill rides, the park also offers a mini-zoo and the Wizard's Village for the younger members of the family. Admission price covers everything but food, including puppet shows, dance revues and other live entertainment.

✉ 26101 Magic Mountain Parkway, off Interstate 5 Freeway, near Valencia ☎ 661/255-4103; www.sixflags.com/parks/magicmountain 🕓 Call for hours

Six Flags Waterworld

This park has some of the best high-speed slides and other water attractions.

✉ Exposition Boulevard, Sacramento ☎ 916/924-0556 🕓 Late May–early Sep; call for hours
✋ Expensive

Top activities

Attending concerts from rock to jazz to classical.

Boating (all kinds).

Cycling – rental of bicycles can be readily arranged.

Exercising at a gym or by doing yoga, pilates or ta'i chi.

Going to the movies – film buffs can catch everything from new releases to classic films.

Golfing in Palm Springs, known as the Winter Golf Capital of the World.

Hiking/backpacking – popular throughout the state.

Rollerblading along the beachfront in Venice Beach.

Surfing in the Pacific.

Visiting the theme parks.

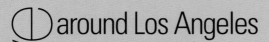

a drive around Los Angeles

This drive winds through some of LA's most exclusive neighborhoods, then west to Malibu.

From the Hollywood Bowl, drive north, veering to the left on to Cahuenga Boulevard. Drive to the Mulholland Drive turn-off, go left and continue on to Mulholland west.

Along Mulholland are several turn-offs for viewing the city and the San Fernando Valley below.

Continue westward on Mulholland to the 405 Freeway, entering southbound.

Take the first exit (Getty Center Drive), the site of the Getty Center (➤ 137).

Continue south on the 405 to Sunset Boulevard and exit. Turn right on to Sunset and drive westward. Continue to Bundy Drive and turn left at the light. Travel south about a mile (1.6km) to reach the stoplight at San Vincente. Go through the light, turn left and right to continue on Bundy.

Just past the next stop-light is the Simpson-Goldman murder scene, to your right.

Return to Sunset and turn left. Travel west on Sunset through the Pacific Palisades, to Pacific Coast Highway, along the ocean.

At the junction of Sunset and the Pacific Coast Highway is Gladstones 4 Fish, a great place to take lunch.

Continue north on Pacific Coast Highway to Malibu. Las Tunas State Beach is a good beach to spend time on. Continue north to Malibu Canyon Road and turn right at the light. Follow the road over the Santa Monica Mountains and turn into Las Virgines Road. Continue to the on-ramp to the 101 Freeway, and follow it south to the Highland exit and the Hollywood Bowl.

Distance 60 miles (97km)
Time About 5 hours
Start/end point Hollywood Bowl
Lunch Gladstones 4 Fish ($$) ✉ 17300 Pacific Coast Highway, Pacific Palisades
☎ 310/454-3474

Exploring

Describing California and its people is like trying to describe a beautiful painting: most people will have a different perspective and feeling. The word that most readily comes to mind is extreme. Nowhere on earth can one find such *extreme* variances of scenic splendor or inhabitants. Within an 80-mile (129km) span are the highest and lowest elevations in the United States, each with its own unique beauty.

From the very first person to set foot in the state to its most recent émigré, the trait that has most greatly characterized the state's populace is a deep commitment to adventure. California seems to define the concept of diversity with both its geography and its inhabitants. With nearly every culture represented throughout the state, there are enough dining and entertainment selections to suit everyone's desire.

San Francisco

The Gold Rush of the mid-19th century brought a diverse ethnicity to San Francisco. Areas like Chinatown and North Beach have preserved their different native cultures.

Out in the bay to the north is the infamous Alcatraz Island, the site of the notorious former prison. It is easily seen from Coit Tower, on top of Telegraph Hill. Russian Hill provides a panoramic look at the Golden Gate Bridge and the bay. To the north and east of the city lie the Napa Valley and Marin County, where wine-tasting is the hobby of choice.

Few places in the world can boast, as San Francisco can, the sophistication of a major metropolitan area, while also being offset by 42 hills and, at the same time, surrounded by the serenity of lush vineyards.

ALCATRAZ

Of the 14 islands punctuating the massive San Francisco Bay,
12-acre (5ha) Alcatraz is the most famous. Rising 135ft (41m)
out of the bay, it is easy to see why it is nicknamed "The Rock."
Although wild flowers are abundant on the island and the views of
the bay and the Golden Gate bridge are breathtaking, most visitors
visit the island to tour the massive fortress that covers most of the
grounds. Built in 1858 as a military
post, it soon became a military prison
and finally a federal penitentiary.

Because of the severe tides and
undertow of the surrounding chilly
waters, escape from the prison was
reputed to be impossible. Three
inmates dug their way out of their
prison cells and disappeared in 1962.
No one knows if they made it to the
mainland, but their bodies were never
found. The prison closed soon after the
attempt, and a group of Native
Americans claimed the island as their
birthright. Some of the buildings were
burned before the National Park Service took control and reopened
Alcatraz as a tourist attraction in 1973.

Three prominent movies have been filmed on the island: *Escape from Alcatraz*, *The Birdman of Alcatraz* and *The Rock*. Tours include a close-up look at the cells with audio-cassette narration by former prisoners and guards and exterior trail walks led by park rangers. Dress warmly and wear comfortable shoes.

www.alcatrazcruises.com

🚩 *San Francisco 2a (off map)* ☎ 415/981-7625 🕐 Hours vary, advance reservations recommended ✋ Moderate ⛴ Ferry from Pier 41, Fisherman's Wharf

ASIAN ART MUSEUM

More than 40 Asian countries are represented in this museum, the largest of its kind outside the Asian continent. Exclusive to this museum are works of Asian art spanning 4,000 years of Chinese history. It also houses outstanding exhibits from India, Japan and Korea and more than 300 works from the estates of Chinese emperors.

www.asianart.org

🚩 *San Francisco 2f* ✉ 200 Larkin Street, Civic Center ☎ 415/581-3500 🕐 Tue–Sun 10–5, Thu 10–9 ✋ Moderate, free 1st Tue of month

CABLE CAR MUSEUM AND POWERHOUSE VIEWING GALLERY

If you're fascinated by San Francisco's cable-cars, visit this working nerve center and museum. On exhibit are the first cable-cars, which went unchanged for almost 100 years. Their design was modernized in 1982. Also housed in the three-level, red-brick 1907 barn are photographs, artifacts and a model collection. From the viewing gallery you can watch craftsmen working on the cars.

✚ *San Francisco 3d* ✉ 1201 Mason Street ☎ 415/474-1887 ◷ Daily 10–5 (extended hours in spring and summer) ✋ Free

CALIFORNIA ACADEMY OF SCIENCES

Dating back to the mid-19th century, this is considered one of the finest natural history museums in the world. It houses several galleries, an exhibit that allows visitors to "experience" an earthquake, and a hands-on Discovery Room for children. The Steinhart Aquarium has almost 14,000 salt-water species which include octopuses, sea-horses, dolphins and sharks. The ANTS exhibit showcases the nest-building and food-collecting behavior of six live ant colonies. The Howard Street location also has a nurturing place called the Nature Nest for young visitors. Note: The Academy has moved to temporary premises in Howard Street and is expected to return to Golden Gate Park in 2008.

🚩 *San Francisco 4f* ✉ 875 Howard Street, between 4th and 5th streets
☎ 415/750-7145 🕐 Daily 10–5 (extended hours in summer) 👆 Moderate; senior/children rates. Free 1st Wed of month

CALIFORNIA PALACE OF THE LEGION OF HONOR

Refurbished in 1995, this classical palace was inspired by the Hotel de Salm in Paris, the site where Napoleon established the Legion D'Honneur. The Palace houses an extraordinary collection of 75,000 prints and drawings from the Achenbach Foundation, and expansive European art dating from 2500BC through to the 20th century. Rodin's *The Thinker* is on display in the courtyard.

🚩 *San Francisco 1d (off map)* ✉ 34th Avenue and Clement Street, Lincoln Park ☎ 415/750-3600 🕐 Tue–Sun 9:30–5 👆 Moderate; senior/children rates; free every Tue

CARTOON ART MUSEUM

This museum houses permanent and rotating exhibits of original two- and three-dimensional art and cartoon artifacts. You can see the original artwork and drawings used in the production of cartoons. Some exhibits go back to the 18th century. Video presentations are also part of the program.

www.cartoonart.org

✚ *San Francisco 4e* ✉ 655 Mission Street ☎ 415/227-8666 🕓 Tue–Sun 11–5. Closed public hols 🖐 *Moderate; senior/children rates*

CHINESE HISTORICAL SOCIETY OF AMERICA

The largest collection of Chinese-American artifacts in the US is housed here, including Chinese dragon heads, an 1880 Buddhist altar and a concise history of the Chinese experience in America, from 1840 to the present day.

✚ *San Francisco 3d* ✉ 965 Clay Street ☎ 415/391-1188 🕓 Tue–Fri noon–5, Sat–Sun noon–4 🖐 *Inexpensive*

CIVIC CENTER PLAZA

Dominated by the French Renaissance-inspired City Hall, the complex dates back to the 1906 earthquake. On the west end is the War Memorial and Performing Arts Center. The Center is home to the Louise M. Davies Symphony Hall, the War Memorial Opera House and the War Memorial Veterans Building. The latter contains the San Francisco Museum of Modern Art and the Herbst Theatre, where the United Nations charter was signed in 1945. Other classically styled buildings in the plaza complex are the Civic Auditorium, the San Francisco Public Library and the State Building.

✚ *San Francisco 2f* ✉ Van Ness Avenue/Polk Street at Grove and McAllister streets ☎ 415/557-4266 (information) 🖐 *Free*

DE YOUNG MUSEUM

An extensive collection of American artwork is contained in this 22-gallery complex set in Golden Gate Park. The museum's exhibits include paintings, sculpture, decorative arts, textiles and furniture. Some of the artwork dates to the mid-17th century. Also on display are classical and tribal works.

✚ *San Francisco 1f (off map)* ✉ 2501 Irving Street (at 26th Avenue)
☎ 415/750-3600 🕐 Tue–Sat 10–4:45 ✋ Free

FISHERMAN'S WHARF

Bustling Fisherman's Wharf is the center of San Francisco's thriving tourist trade. It has many shops, street stands, food emporia and the like. Originally, it was an active base for San Francisco Bay's once busy fishing industry, until the late 1940s. A small fleet still operates.

✚ *San Francisco 2a* ✉ North of North Beach 🍴 Cafés, stands ($)

a walk around Chinatown

This walk takes you through the largest Chinese community outside Asia.

Enter through the Chinatown Gate, at Bush Street and Grant Avenue.

Note the dragon-entwined lampposts and pagoda roofs as you are greeted by a cacophony of Chinese street merchants and the aromas of simmering noodles.

Walk north on Grant to the Dragon House Antiques (No 455).

Continue up Grant to St. Mary's Park where there's a 12ft (3.5m) sculpture of Sun Yat-sen.

Continue north to Clay, turn right to Kearny, then left to Portsmouth Square. Across Kearny is the Holiday Inn.

Pop inside to the Chinese Cultural Center.

Go north on Kearny, to Pacific, then left to the New Asia restaurant (No 772), a good choice for lunch. Continue west on Pacific to Grant, then go left two blocks to Washington. Turn right.

Admire the three-tiered pagoda-style Bank of Canton, then continue west to the Tien Hou Temple (in Waverly Place on Washington). Around the corner is The Great China Herb Co. (No 857), where sellers fill herbal prescriptions.

Continue west on Washington to Stockton, then turn left.

The Chinese Six Companies building (No 843) is an architectural wonder, with its curved roof tiles and elaborate cornices.

Walk south on Stockton to the Stockton Street Tunnel. A 15-minute walk through the tunnel brings you to downtown Union Square.

Distance 5 miles (8km)
Time 2–4 hours
Start point Chinatown Gate ✚ *San Francisco 4d*
End point Union Square ✚ *San Francisco 3e*
Lunch New Asia ($$) ✉ 772 Pacific Avenue ☎ 415/391-6666

GOLDEN GATE BRIDGE AND NATIONAL RECREATION AREA

Best places to see, pages 42–43.

GRACE CATHEDRAL

Taking over a half-century to build, this marvelous structure is a near-perfect replica of a Florentine cathedral. The singing of the Vespers each Thursday at 5:15pm is a truly spiritual experience.

✚ *San Francisco 2d* ✉ 1100 California Street ☎ 415/749-6300 🖐 Free, but donations accepted

HYDE STREET PIER AND HISTORICAL SHIPS

In the Fisherman's Wharf area, this pier is the permanent home of several historical ships. Here you will find the ferry boat *Eureka* (1890), once the world's largest ferry boat, and the *Balclutha*, a square-rigged sailing ship from Scotland (1886), famed for rounding Cape Horn several times. Before leaving the area, drop into the National Maritime Museum at nearby Aquatic Park.

San Francisco 1a 415/561-7100 Daily 10–5 Inexpensive. National Park Golden Eagle Pass free

LOMBARD STREET

Located in the Russian Hill district, this is San Francisco's famous "crookedest" street. Traffic zigzags down it at 5mph (8kph), moving around colorful gardens which were established in the 1920s.

San Francisco 1b–4b Between Hyde and Leavenworth streets

MISSION SAN FRANCISCO DE ASIS

Founded in 1776 and moved to its present site in 1782, the mission is thought to be the oldest standing structure in the city. Adjoining is the Mission Dolores Basilica, the least changed of all California's existing missions. The architecture of Mission Dolores is a combination of Moorish, Mission and Corinthian styles, and the garden cemetery is filled with the burial sites of San Francisco pioneers.

✚ *San Francisco 2f (off map)* ✉ 16th and Dolores streets ☎ 415/621-8203 🕐 Daily 9–4:30 (until 4 in fall and winter) 🖐 Inexpensive

NORTH BEACH

This thriving, trendy neighborhood, on the northeastern tip of San Francisco, is bound by Chinatown, the Financial District and Russian Hill. North Beach has a distinctly Italian atmosphere, and is central to most attractions, shops and restaurants in the area. Its heyday in the 1950s saw Jack Kerouac and other Beat Generation

poets frequenting the cafés and bookstores, which remain
important cultural meeting places. At the center of the
neighborhood is **Coit Tower**, an impressive 210ft (64m) landmark,
built in 1934, reached on foot via the Filbert Steps by Darnell Place.

✚ *San Francisco 3b*

Coit Tower

☎ 415/362 0808 🕓 Daily 10–6:30 ✋ Inexpensive (to go to top of tower)

PALACE OF FINE ARTS

This Bernard Maybeck Greco-
Romanesque rotunda is one of
the most photographed buildings
in San Francisco. Levelled by the
great earthquake of 1906, it was
completely rebuilt in 1915 and
today presents continuing cultural
events. Inside the complex is the
Exploratorium, a wonderful
hands-on science museum, ideal
for families, with toys disguised
as science education.

✚ *San Francisco 1b (off map)*

✉ 3601 Lyon Street ☎ 415/561-0360

🕓 Tue–Sun 10–5; open on Mon hols ✋ Moderate, free 1st Wed of month

ST MARY'S CATHEDRAL OF THE ASSUMPTION

The radical architecture by Pietro Belluschi and Pier Luigi Nervi
caused great debate during construction. Rising on concrete
pylons to a height of 190ft (58m), the exterior resembles a
washing machine agitator. Inside, however, the soaring cruciform
is nothing short of breathtaking. The majestic pipe organ, itself, is
worth seeing.

✚ *San Francisco 1e* ✉ 1111 Gough Street ☎ 415/567-2020 🕓 Mon–Fri
7–5, Sun 7–6:30 ✋ Free, but donations accepted

SAN FRANCISCO MUSEUM OF MODERN ART

Devoted solely to modern art and occupying a quarter-million sq ft, this is the main structure in the Yerba Buena Arts Center (SoMo district). Exhibits include a world-renowned collection of photography, and 20th-century works from such artists as Dali, O'Keefe and Jasper Johns. A current feature exhibit is "From Matisse to Diebenkorn: Works from the Permanent Collection."

✚ *San Francisco 4e* ✉ 151 Third Street
☎ 415/357-4000 🕐 Mon, Tue, Fri–Sun 11–5:45; Thu 11–8:45 ✋ Moderate, senior/student rates, free 1st Tue of month

TRANSAMERICA PYRAMID

Depending on who you ask, this structure is either a landmark or an eyesore. Completed in 1972, the pyramid skyscraper juts 853ft (260m) skyward, making it the tallest building in San Francisco.

✚ *San Francisco 4d* ✉ 600 Montgomery Street
🕐 Mon–Fri 8–4

UNION STREET

Union Street runs east–west from Montgomery Street in North
Beach to the Presidio. It is one of the city's most fashionable
areas in which to live and shop, with its many beautifully restored
Victorian mansions that have been converted into boutiques, art
galleries and cafés. Scattered among the bustling retail spots are
several landmarks. The **Octagon House** (just off Union Street) is
a pale-blue, eight-sided structure that features antique furniture
from the 18th and 19th centuries. Also of interest is an exhibit
containing the signatures of 54 of the 56 original signatories of
the Declaration of Independence.

✚ *San Francisco 2c–4b*

Octagon House

✉ 2645 Gough Street ☎ 415/441-7512 🕐 2nd and 4th Thu and 2nd Sun
of each month (except Jan), noon–3. Closed public hols ✋ Contributions

WELLS FARGO HISTORY MUSEUM

The Wells Fargo History Museum connects the Wells Fargo
Bank's history to the Gold Rush, historic San Francisco and stage
coach travel in early California.

Henry Wells and William
Fargo started Wells Fargo &
Co in 1852, providing express
and banking services to the
'49ers. Visitors can see an
original stage coach and rare
gold coins and nuggets, work
a telegraph, and learn about
the people who built the
West.

✚ *San Francisco 4d* ✉ 420
Montgomery Street ☎ 415/396-
2619 🕐 Mon–Fri 9–5. Closed
public hols ✋ Free

HOTELS

☝☝☝ Archbishop's Mansion ($$)
Historic 1904 bed-and-breakfast with stained-glass windows and elegant European furnishings.
✉ 1000 Fulton Street ☎ 415/563-7872; www.jduhospitality.com

☝☝ Comfort Inn by the Bay ($)
Near Lombard Street and the major attractions. Reasonable rates.
✉ 2775 Van Ness Avenue ☎ 415/928-5000

☝☝☝☝ The Fairmont San Francisco ($$$)
Newly renovated historic hotel, situated atop Nob Hill.
✉ 950 Mason Street ☎ 415/772-5000; www.fairmont.com/sanfrancisco

Four Season's Clift ($$$)
This art deco hotel is one of the city's most famous. Oriental carpets, chandeliers and tasteful rooms.
✉ 495 Geary Street ☎ 415/775-4700; www.clifthotel.com

☝☝☝ Hotel Triton ($$)
Near Chinatown. Tasteful art deco design with exhibitions of local artwork in the lobby.
✉ 342 Grant Avenue ☎ 415/394-0500; www.hoteltriton.com

☝☝☝ The Inn at the Opera
Near Performing Arts Center. Small and elegant with first-rate service.
✉ 333 Fulton Street ☎ 415/863-8400; www.innattheopera.com

☝☝ ☝☝ Mark Hopkins Inter-Continental ($$$)
On the site of the old Mark Hopkins mansion. Offers a spectacular view of the city.
✉ 1 Nob Hill ☎ 415/392-3434; www.intercontinental.com

☝☝☝ Mill Valley Inn ($$)
Beautiful stucco hotel at the center of this small, artistic community.

✉ 165 Throckmorton Avenue, Mill Valley ☎ 415/389-6608;
www.millvalleyinn.com

▼▼▼ Queen Anne ($$)
Converted Victorian house, impressive for its art deco style.
Complimentary breakfast, and afternoon tea and sherry.
✉ 1590 Sutter Street ☎ 415/441-2828; www.queenanne.com

▼▼▼ Sir Francis Drake ($$)
Opulence with bed-and-breakfast flavor.
✉ 450 Powell Street ☎ 415/392-7755; www.sirfrancisdrake.com

▼▼▼ York Hotel ($$)
Renovated 1922 hotel with marble floors. Parts of Alfred
Hitchcock's Vertigo were filmed here.
✉ 940 Sutter Street ☎ 415/885-6800; www.yorkhotel.com

RESTAURANTS

▼▼▼ Alfred's Steakhouse ($$)
Quintessential steakhouse with bordello-like setting. Big portions.
✉ 659 Merchant Street, between Kearny and Montgomery streets 415/781-7058 ⊙ Lunch, dinner

▼▼▼ Aqua ($$$)
Glamorous downtown restaurant specializing in French-American
gourmet seafood.
✉ 252 California Street ☎ 415/956-9662 ⊙ Lunch, dinner

▼▼▼ Balboa Cafe ($$)
Trendy café with a traditional American menu. The place to "see
and be seen."
✉ 3199 Fillmore Street ☎ 415/921-3944 ⊙ Lunch, dinner

▼▼ Betelnut ($$)
Lively atmosphere, tropical drinks and pan-Asion fare, with
elements of Thai, Chinese and Korean cuisine.
✉ 2030 Union Street ☎ 415/929-8855 ⊙ Lunch, dinner

▼▼▼ Bix ($$$)

Martinis, cigar smoke, upscale crowd and great steaks and seafood make this one of San Francisco's most popular restaurants. Reservations recommended.

✉ 56 Gold Street, between Montgomery and Sansome streets ☎ 415/433-6300 🕔 Dinner; lunch Fri only

Café 2223 Restaurant and Bar ($$)

Trendy California cuisine and lively cocktails. Serves an excellent weekend brunch.

✉ 2223 Market Street ☎ 415/431-0692 🕔 Brunch, lunch, dinner

▼▼▼ Le Charm ($$)

French bistro and garden for indoor or outdoor dining, with terrific prix fixe menu.

✉ 315 5th Street ☎ 415/546-6128 🕔 Lunch, dinner

Dottie's True Blue Cafe ($)

See page 58.

Ebisu ($$)

Top-rated sushi and traditional Asian food. You may have to wait but its worth it.

✉ 1283 Ninth Avenue ☎ 415/566-1770 🕔 Lunch, dinner

Firefly ($$)

Local favorite for home cooking and friendly service. Great place to people watch.

✉ 4288 24th Street ☎ 415/821-7652 🕔 Lunch, dinner

▼▼▼ ▼▼▼ Fleur de Lys ($$$)

The city's most romantic restaurant. Attentive service and superb contemporary French food.

✉ 777 Sutter Street ☎ 415/673-7779 🕔 Lunch, dinner; closed Sun

❦❦ Fog City Diner ($$)

Upscale '50s-style diner on Telegraph Hill. American and seafood specialties.

✉ 1300 Battery Street ☎ 415/982-2000 🕐 Lunch, dinner

❦❦❦❦❦ Gary Danko ($$$)

Romantic Russian Hill/wharf restaurant featuring French-Californian fare. Diners can design their own three- to five-course meal. Pricey, but worth it.

✉ 800 N Point Street ☎ 415/749-2060 🕐 Dinner only

❦❦❦ Jeanty at Jack's ($$)

Opened in 1864, this historic restaurant has a new owner and a new French menu.

✉ 615 Sacramento Street ☎ 415/693-0941 🕐 Lunch, dinner

Kate's Kitchen ($)

Authentic, inexpensive "soul" food in the famous Haight-Ashbury district. Great for breakfast or late-night dining.

✉ 471 Haight Street ☎ 415/626-3984 🕐 Breakfast, lunch, dinner; no credit cards

❦❦❦ Lu Lu ($$)

Innovative, Mediterranean bistro located in a large converted warehouse. Family-style service with excellent food.

✉ 816 Folsom ☎ 415/495-5775 🕐 Lunch, dinner

The Mandarin ($$$)

Long-time favorite for great views and exotic environment. Chinese cuisine; specializes in Peking duck.

✉ 900 N Point Street ☎ 415/673-8812 🕐 Lunch, dinner

Mel's Drive In ($)

A revival of the popular 1950s-style drive-in. Top-rated burgers, fries and milk shakes and, of course, a great jukebox.

✉ 2165 Lombard Street ☎ 415/921-2867 ✉ 3355 Geary Street ☎ 415/387 2244 ✉ 801 Mission Street ☎ 415/227-4477 🕐 Lunch, dinner, open late

Original Joe's ($)
Italian and American cooking in a great setting.
✉ 144 Taylor Street ☎ 415/775-4877 ⏰ Lunch, dinner

♦♦ L'Osteria del Forno ($$)
Northern Italian cuisine in North Beach. Expect a long wait, as the restaurant is tiny and the food delicious.
✉ 519 Columbus Avenue ☎ 415/982-1124 ⏰ Lunch, dinner; closed Tue; no credit cards

♦♦ Perry's ($)
Local watering hole, very popular with the young set. Good American food, comfortable ambience.
✉ 185 Sutter Street ☎ 415/989-6895 ⏰ Lunch, dinner

♦♦♦ Plumpjack Cafe ($$)
"Hot spot" specializing in American food. Top-notch wine list. Reservations may be difficult to get, but it's worth persisting.
✉ 3127 Fillmore Street ☎ 415/563-4755 ⏰ Lunch, dinner

♦♦♦ Slanted Door ($$$)
Creative Vietnamese food accompanied by a fantastic view of the Bay Bridge.
✉ Ferry Building, 1 Ferry Plaza ☎ 415/861-8032 ⏰ Lunch, dinner

Swan Oyster Depot ($$)
Unique seafood emporium in operation since 1912. Service from an old-fashioned marble bar.
✉ 1517 Polk Street ☎ 415/673-1101 ⏰ Lunch, dinner; closed Sun; no credit cards

SHOPPING

ART AND ANTIQUES
Fillmore Street
Specialty shops include book and music stores, and clothing from retro to new fashion.
✉ Jackson and Sutter

The Japan Center
Art galleries and Oriental gift shops, interspersed with sushi bars and tea houses.

✉ Bounded by Laguna, Geary, Fillmore, Sutter and Post streets

CRAFTS
Fisherman's Wharf
There are four shopping centers here – Pier 39, The Cannery, Ghirardelli Square and The Anchorage. See also page 63.

✉ Columbus on the Bay

FASHION
Haight Street
Famous for hippies in the 1960s; some shops still sell offbeat, vintage clothes. Book and music shops.

✉ At Ashbury Street

SoMa
Popular for bargain stores, night-spots and cafés.

✉ South of Market Street

Union Square
Large department stores are Macy's, Neiman-Marcus and Saks Fifth Avenue.

✉ Downtown ☎ Macy's 415/397-3333; Neiman-Marcus 415/362-3900; Saks Fifth Avenue 415/986-4300

Union Street
One of the best streets in San Francisco, with specialist shops/galleries.

✉ Between Gough and Steiner

PRODUCE
Chinatown
Almost as fun as finding unique produce and great bargains is watching the locals wrangle for better prices. See also page 63.

✉ Bordered by Broadway, Bush, Kearny and Powell streets

STORES

The Embarcadero Center

Shops, restaurants, offices, hotels in a huge downtown complex.

✉ Sacramento and Clay streets 🚇 BART, Muni

Ghirardelli Square

Formerly a chocolate factory, this area has become a chic center of stores and top restaurants.

✉ At Fisherman's Wharf

ENTERTAINMENT

American Conservatory Theater (ACT)

One of the top regional theaters in the US.

✉ 415 Geary Street ☎ 415/749-2228

Bottom of the Hill

Alternative bands head to this Potrero Hill club, which has a beer garden, pool tables and also serves food.

✉ 1233 17th Street ☎ 415/621-4455 (information line)

111 Minna

An art gallery that does double duty as a DJ/dance venue in the evenings.

✉ 111 Minna Street, at 2nd Street ☎ 415/974-1719

Louise M. Davies Symphony Hall

Symphonies, concerts; also tours of this stream-lined glass-and-granite building.

✉ Van Ness Avenue and Grove Street, Civic Center ☎ 415/864-6000

Orpheum Theatre

The largest touring shows to San Francisco play here.

✉ 1192 Market Street ☎ 415/551-2000

Vesuvio Cafe

This former haunt of Beat poets hasn't changed much in 30 years.

✉ 255 Columbus Avenue ☎ 415/362-3370

Northern California

Some of California's most beautiful areas can be found in the north of the state. The Monterey Peninsula and Big Sur coastlines are possibly the most scenic in the country, and San Francisco, with its rich cultural diversity, one of the most fascinating.

Yosemite National Park, Lake Tahoe and the Wine Country all share qualities of untouched beauty. The northern coastline is the

least populated and is a perfect contrast to the busy beach areas to the south. Nowhere can you find natural beauty like that of the Redwood National Forest, which is said to contain the world's tallest tree.

Silicon Valley, south of San Francisco, is the center of the country's computer and electronics industries, and Sacramento is the state capitol and center of government.

EUREKA

Eureka is the largest town on California's northernmost coast. Set along Humboldt Bay, it is home to an impressive fishing fleet. Its name, from the Greek word for "I have found it," refers to the cries from many gold miners (called '49ers) in the 19th century. The Old Town section is worth a visit for its elegantly refurbished Victorian homes.

The old 1912 building, once the town's main bank, now houses the **Clarke Memorial Museum.** It houses an excellent collection of California Native American historic artifacts.

Blue Ox Millworks is a working mill that includes a blacksmith shop and a re-creation of a logging camp. **Sequoia Park,** a beautiful grove of virgin redwoods in 52 acres (21ha), has a formal flower garden, duck pond, and deer and elk paddocks.

✚ 2C

Clarke Memorial Museum

✉ 240 E Street ☎ 707/443-947 🕐 Tue–Sat 11–4 ✋ Free

Blue Ox Millworks

✉ Foot of X Street ☎ 707/444-3437 🕐 Mon–Fri 9–5, Sat by appointment ✋ Inexpensive

Sequoia Park

✉ 3414 W Street ☎ 707/442-6552 🕐 Daily 10–5 ✋ Inexpensive 🍴 Picnic facilities

GOLD COUNTRY TOWNS

Also known as the Mother Lode Country, this scenic area extends 300 miles (484km) along Highway 49, through the western Sierra

Nevada foothills. Once the thriving Old West, it is now mostly ghost towns, several of which are open to tourists.

Angel's Camp Museum, in Angel's Camp (➤ 102), was the center for gravel and quartz mining in 1849. You can see photographs, relics and 3 acres (1.21ha) of old mining equipment from the old days.

Marshall Gold Discovery State Historic Park is where James Marshall discovered gold. The drive-through park features a replica of Sutter's Mill and memorial statue and grave site of James Marshall.

The Empire Mine State Historic Park (➤ 103), 2 miles (3.5km) east of Grass Valley, is the Gold Country's best preserved quartz mining operation. During the boom years, the 367 miles (592km) of mine shafts produced six million ounces of gold.

Mercer Caverns, 1 mile (1.6km) north of Murphys, via Main Street, were discovered in 1885 by Walter Mercer, a gold prospector. The 45-minute tour gives the opportunity to view the enormous stalagmites and stalactites close up.

➕ 6G
Angel's Camp Museum
✉ 753 South Main Street ☎ 209/736-2963
🕐 Mar–end Dec daily 10–3; Jan–end Feb Sat, Sun 10–3 ✋ Inexpensive
Marshall Gold Discovery State Historic Park
✉ South fork of the American River and Highway 49, Coloma ☎ 530/622-3470 🕐 Museum daily 10–3; park 8–sunset ✋ Inexpensive

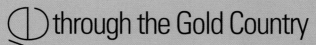 through the Gold Country

This drive will take you through Gold Country along historic Highway 49.

Begin in Mariposa, where SR 49 meets SR 140.

Here you can visit the California State Mining and Mineral Museum and the Mariposa County Museum.

Proceed north on SR 49 to Chinese Camp and the State Historic Park. A few miles north is Jamestown.

Jamestown served as a backdrop for the film *High Noon* and the television series *Little House on the Prairie*.

Follow 49 north, stopping in Tuttletown.

You can view a replica of Mark Twain's cabin on Jackass Hill (Tuttletown was originally called Jackass Gulch).

Continue to Columbia.

Here you can try your hand at panning for gold, or ride an authentic stagecoach.

Continue north on 49 to Angel's Camp.

This is where Mark Twain first heard the "jumping frog" story from bartender Ben Coon. If you are here in May, don't miss the frog jumping contest. The foundation of Angel's Mine is across from the Catholic Church.

Continue north to Jackson and Placerville.

Jackson was once home of the Mohawk Indians, and

Placerville was formerly known as "Hangtown." Gold Bug Mine is worth a visit.

Farther north are Coloma, Auburn and Grass Valley.

The latter is home to Empire Mine State Historic Park (▶ 101) and North Star Mine Museum, both offering tours.

The drive ends in Nevada City.

Distance Approximately 100 miles (162km)
Time 8 hours
Start point Mariposa ✚ 7R
End point Nevada City ✚ 5E
Lunch National Hotel Restaurant ($) ✉ 18183 Main Street, Jamestown ☎ 209/984-3446

LAKE TAHOE

Situated on the California–Nevada stateline, Lake Tahoe is one of the most popular resort communities in the state. Although this beautiful lake is 6,228ft (1,899m) above sea level, it never freezes because of its depth. You will find top-notch ski facilities here, and in summer, water sports include lake cruises, water skiing and sailing.

For a spectacular aerial view of the entire area, including the site of the 1960 Winter Olympic Games, ride the gondola to the top of the Squaw Valley Ski Area.

✚ 7N

Squaw Valley Cable Car

✉ 1960 Squaw Valley Road, Olympic Valley ☎ 530/583-6985 🕐 Call to check. Closed mid-Oct to Dec 1 ✋ Moderate

LASSEN VOLCANIC NATIONAL PARK

Lassen Park stretches over 100,000 acres (40,486ha) in the northeastern corner of California, where the Cascade and Sierra Nevada mountains meet. Highlights are Lassen Peak, Cinder Cone, Prospect Peak and Mount Harkness, the latter two volcanoes topped by cinder cones.

Lassen's numerous volcanic eruptions subsided in 1921 and have been replaced by hot springs and lakes, lava flows and mudpots, all linked together by hiking trails that lead to the summit and back.

➕ 5C ✉ 9 miles (15km) east of Mineral, via SR 36
☎ 530/595-4444 🕐 Year-round

MAMMOTH LAKES RECREATION AREA

This giant popular resort area in the Inyo National Forest has world-class skiing, and in summertime it's a mountain biking mecca. There is also good camping, fishing and horseback riding here. Hike to the 101ft (31m) Rainbow Falls, or visit the Devil's Postpile National Monument, 60ft (18m) multisided columns that are by-products of former volcanic activity.

➕ 9Q 🍴 Restaurants ($$)
ℹ Chamber of Commerce, PO Box 48, Mammoth Lakes, 93546 ☎ 760/934-2712
🕐 Mon–Fri 9–5

MENDOCINO

Mendocino, off scenic US 1, is perhaps the most charming small town in California. It is noted for its Cape Cod and Victorian-style architecture and its active, artistic community. The entire town is on the National Register of Historic Places. Film buffs will recognize it from such films as *The Summer of '42*, *East of Eden* and television's *Murder She Wrote*. The Art Center is the epicenter of the many art museums in the community, and includes galleries, live theater and arts and craft fairs.

www.mendocinocoast.com

✚ 2E

Mendocino Art Center

✉ 45200 Little Lake Street ☎ 707/937-5818 or 800/653-3328 🕐 Call for times 💷 Moderate

ℹ Mendocino Chamber of Commerce ✉ 332 North Main Street ☎ 707/961-6300 🕐 Daily 10–4

MODESTO

This quintessential California town was made famous by George Lucas's film *American Graffiti*. Near the center of the state, it is the home of the Blue Diamond Almonds company.

The **McHenry Museum** re-creates a 19th-century school, blacksmith shop, kitchen, country store and others with changing exhibits. The **McHenry Mansion,** a block away, exhibits antique furnishings and artwork in a restored Victorian home.

✚ 5H

McHenry Museum & Mansion

✉ 1402 "I" Street ☎ 209/577-5366 (museum); 209/577-5341 (mansion) 🕐 Tue–Sun noon–4. Closed major holidays 💷 Free, donations requested ❓ Tours of mansion offered Sun–Thu 1–4, Fri noon–3

MOUNT SHASTA

Spiritual-minded Californians flock to this mountain because it is said to be a "vortex of spiritual energy." For the more earthbound there is hiking, climbing, and skiing in winter. Several surrounding lakes offer waterside camping, fishing and watersports, including skating in winter. The **Mount Shasta State Fish Hatchery,** in the center of the area, produces 5 to 10 million trout annually to stock Northern California lakes.

➕ 4B

Mount Shasta State Fish Hatchery

☎ 530/926-2215 🕐 Daily 7am–dusk ✋ Free

ℹ Chamber of Commerce Visitors Bureau ✉ 300 Pine Street ☎ 800/926-4865; www.mtshastachamber.com 🕐 Daily 9:30–5:30

NAPA VALLEY
Best places to see, pages 50–51.

NATURAL BRIDGES STATE BEACH
Set in 65 acres (26ha), this beach, just before Santa Cruz, is a wonderful place to observe the migration of the colorful Monarch butterfly between mid-October and February. There are also tide pools to explore, as well as ecological and wildlife exhibits in the visitor center.

➕ 4J ✉ West Cliff Drive ☎ 831/423-4609 🕓 Beach daily 8–dusk; visitor center 10–4 ✋ Inexpensive

OAKLAND
Linked to San Francisco by the Bay Bridge, Oakland has long suffered from its close proximity to the city across the bay. In

reality, it is a culturally rich and diversified town and has counted among its famous citizens Jack London and Gertrude Stein. **Oakland Museum** has an extensive collection of historical and contemporary art housed in the Gallery of California Art. The museum is one of the best in the state for studying the diverse cultural make-up and subsequent historical progress.

Lake Merritt, created in the late 19th century by the damming of a section of the Oakland estuary, was one of the first natural wildlife preserves established in the US.

➕ 4H

Oakland Museum

✉ 10th and Oak Street ☎ 510/238-2200 🕑 Wed–Sat 10–5, Sun noon–5
✋ Inexpensive

PETALUMA

Petaluma is another one of the quintessential small California towns. Situated on the Petaluma River, it has retained most of its 19th-century architecture and, like Modesto (➤ 106), has become a favorite for filming television series and movies. *American Graffiti* and *Peggy Sue Got Married* were both filmed here.

Philanthropist Andrew Carnegie endowed $12,500 toward the construction of the **Historical Museum/Library** in 1903. It houses permanent and rotating exhibits of early 19th-century Petaluma.

➕ 3G

Petaluma Historical Museum/Library

✉ 20 4th Street ☎ 707/778-4398 🕑 Wed–Sat 10–4, Sun noon–3
✋ Inexpensive

REDWOOD NATIONAL PARK

Best places to see, pages 52–53.

SACRAMENTO

Sacramento was once a major supply center for the California '49ers (gold seekers); now it is the state capital. The names of 5,822 Californians killed in the Vietnam War are engraved on the 22 black granite panels of the California Vietnam Veterans Memorial, near the State Capitol Park.

The exquisite **Governor's Mansion** dates from the 1800s and is now a museum of Victoriana. Items from former governors include a 1902 Steinway piano and Persian carpets.

The Historic Paddlewheeler ***Spirit of Sacramento*** is available for a Sacramento River cruise or special events. The boat's murder-mystery trips are especially popular.

A million-dollar gold collection, ethnic photos and a historic print shop are just some of the items in the five separate areas of the **Discovery Museum.** The **California State Railroad Museum** has three entire floors devoted to railroad-related exhibits, including train cars and 21 locomotives.

Noted for its 210ft (64m) dome, the **State Capitol** building is nearly 150 years old, and is open daily for tours. Adobe-style **Sutter's Fort** was the first European outpost in California and contains some interesting period relics.

Sacramento Zoo has a large reptile display and 350 species of wild animals.

The Towe Ford Museum and Six Flags Waterworld (➤ 69) are also worth visiting.

➕ 5G

Governor's Mansion State Historic Park

✉ 16th and "H" streets ☎ 916/323-3047 🕐 Daily 10–4 ✋ Inexpensive

Spirit of Sacramento

✉ Old Sacramento's "L" Street Landing ☎ 916/552-2933 🕐 Cruises: lunch, brunch, happy hour, dinner, sunset and sightseeing ✋ Moderate 🍴 Dinner, brunch and happy hour cruises available

Discovery Museum

✉ 101 "I" Street ☎ 916/264-7057 🕐 Summer daily 10–5; winter Tue–Sun 10–5 ✋ Inexpensive

California State Railroad Museum

✉ Second and "I" streets ☎ 916/445-6645; www.californiastaterailroadmuseum.org 🕐 Daily 10–5 ✋ Moderate

State Capitol

✉ Between 10th, 15h, "L" and "N" streets ☎ 916/324-0333 🕐 Tours daily 9–4 ✋ Free

Sutter's Fort

✉ 27th and "L" streets ☎ 916/445-4422 🕐 Daily 10–5 ✋ Inexpensive

Sacramento Zoo

✉ 3930 Westland Park Drive ☎ 916/264-5885; www.saczoo.com 🕐 Daily 9–4 (10–4 Nov–Jan) ✋ Moderate

SAN JOSE

San Jose is the 11th largest city in the US. It was founded in the last quarter of the 18th century as El Pueblo de San Jose, and is the oldest Spanish civilian settlement. From 1849 to 1851 it served as the state's capital.

Kelley Park, apart from being a popular city park with such attractions as Happy Hollow family play area and zoo, also contains the Japanese Friendship Garden and Teahouse and the San Jose Historical Museum.

Babylonian, Sumerian and Assyrian artifacts, mummies, sculptures and more can be found at the **Rosicrucian Egyptian**

Museum and Planetarium. There is also a contemporary art gallery.

The **Winchester Mystery House,** a Victorian mansion and home of eccentric firearms heiress Sarah Winchester, was designed to confuse evil spirits. The layout of the house is so complex, with blind closets, secret passageways, 13 bathrooms and 40 staircases, that even Sarah herself needed a map to find her way around. Over looking the Santa Clara Valley from the 4,209ft (1,283m)summit of Mount Hamilton is the **Lick Observatory.**

➕ 4J

Kelley Park

✉ Senter and Story roads ⏰ Daily 8am to 30 mins before dusk 🍴 Picnic facilities 💵 Inexpensive

Rosicrucian Egyptian Museum and Planetarium

✉ 1342 Naglee Avenue ☎ 408/947-3636 ⏰ Mon–Fri 10–5, Sat–Sun 11–6 💵 Moderate; senior/student rates

Winchester Mystery House

✉ 525 S Winchester Boulevard ☎ 408/247-2101 ⏰ Daily from 9am, closing times vary with time of year 💵 Expensive

Lick Observatory

✉ Mount Hamilton Road ☎ 408/274-5061 ⏰ Mon–Fri 12:30–5, Sat–Sun 10–5 💵 Free 🍴 No nearby food or auto services

SAUSALITO

This is the first small town in Marin County after crossing the Golden Gate Bridge. Once a fishing town, it has unfortunately been overrun with tacky tourist shops and no longer has the great charm of years past.

➕ 3H ✉ 5 miles (8km) north of San Francisco 🚢 Ferry from Ferry Building or Fisherman's Wharf

THE WINE COUNTRY

North of San Francisco lie some of the most lush valleys in all of California, the best known of which are the Napa (► 50–51) and Sonoma Valleys. It is here that California's vintners tend their grape vines and produce the many varied wines known and enjoyed worldwide. Whether you are driving, bicycling, taking the Wine Train or flying over the area in one of the many hot air balloons that offer spectacular views of the verdant, rolling, wine lands, you will never forget your excursion to the Wine Country.

The estates of the wineries are incredible to see. Take one of the guided tours of the processing facilities with their informative, enticing tastings. While the large wineries are the most popular, don't pass up the small, family-owned ones, of which there are many. Most have wines that rival the greats, with more convivial atmospheres.

The Napa Valley Wine Train provides daily excursions through the Napa Valley. The 1917 Pullman Dining Car relives the gracious era of elegant rail travel and distinguished service and makes you feel as if you're riding the Orient Express as the three-hour, 36-mile (58km) trip between Napa and St. Helena allows for a leisurely brunch, lunch or dinner. Many concerns are aired by residents that the wineries are a bit too commercial for the area, but there are rarely complaints from the visitors.

To the west, the Sonoma Valley runs for 15 miles (24km) and is a bit less populated than the Napa Valley. As a rule, the 30 or so wineries here offer more personalized tours, with free tastings and a more relaxed atmosphere. The town of Sonoma itself is a good place to start if you wish to visit the valley. The other center of activity is Santa Rosa, to the north of the region.

The Sonoma Valley is particularly rich in Spanish and Mexican history, so be sure to take note of the area's beautiful architecture.

If you're looking for souvenirs of your visit to California, the on-site gift shops have unique offerings and superb wines they will ship anywhere in the world. The wineries listed are just some of the ones you'll want to explore. *Spotlight's Wine Guide* is a complete guide to the area (☎ 415/898-7908).

✚ 4G

Napa Valley Visitors Bureau
✉ 1310 Napa Town Center, Napa ☎ 707/226-7459; www.napavalley.com
🕐 Hours vary; some tours require reservations

Sonoma Valley Visitors Bureau
✉ 453 1st Street, E Sonoma ☎ 707/996-1090; www.sonomavalley.com
🕐 Daily 9–5

Napa Valley Wine Train
✉ 1275 McKinstry Street, Napa ☎ 707/253-2111 or 800/427-4124
🕐 Year-round 🖐 Expensive, reservations and deposit required

Beringer Vineyards
Beringer was one of the very first wineries to open its cellar doors to visitors. The staff here are especially attentive and knowledgeable in discussing the process of wine-making and its history. There are regular tours throughout the day.
✉ Just north of downtown St. Helena, 2000 Main Street ☎ 707/963-7115; www.beringer.com 🕐 Hours and tours vary, phone for information

Buena Vista Winery

As the site of the first vineyard in the valley, Buena Vista, 2 miles (3km) northeast of Sonoma, has become a historical landmark. Hungarian Count Agoston Haraszthy planted the first vines, and the wine cellars, built in 1857, are the oldest stone cellars in the state. The Tasting Room offers selection of award-winning wines and there is a gift shop, a picnic area, an artists' gallery, self-guided tours and historical presentations.

✉ 18000 Old Winery Road, Sonoma ☎ 707/938-1266; www.buenavistacarneros.com 🕐 Daily 10–5

Kenwood Vineyards

Operating on Jack London's former ranch since 1970, this Sonoma country winery produces Cabernet Sauvignon, Zinfandel, Sauvignon Blanc, Chardonnay, Gewürztraminer, Merlot and Pinot Noir on the estate which is about an hour's drive north of San Francisco. Visitors are welcome to sample up to four wines, which are produced from grapes grown on site and sourced from local vineyards, and can hike and take bicycle rides around the property.

✉ 9592 Sonoma Highway (Highway 12), Kenwood ☎ 707/833-4134; www.kenwoodvineyards.com 🕐 Daily 10–5

YOSEMITE NATIONAL PARK

Best places to see, pages 54–55.

HOTELS

EUREKA
☞☞☞ Best Western Humboldt Bay Inn ($)
Remodeled lodging near Humboldt State Park.
✉ 232 W 5th Street ☎ 707/443-2234

LAKE TAHOE
☞☞☞ Best Western Station House Inn ($$)
Central to the lake, with great sporting activities.
✉ 901 Park Avenue, South Lake Tahoe ☎ 530/542-1101

MAMMOTH LAKES
☞☞☞ Mammoth Mountain Inn ($$$)
Resort complex; free transportation to the ski areas. Horseback riding and hiking/hunting trails are on offer.
✉ 1 Minaret Road ☎ 760/934-2581; www.mammothmountain.com

MENDOCINO
☞☞ Headlands Inn Bed & Breakfast ($$)
Remodeled 1868 Victorian with six rooms and one private cottage.
✉ Howard and Albion streets ☎ 707/937-4431; www.headlandsinn.com

MOUNT SHASTA
☞☞☞ Best Western Tree House ($$)
Terrific views of the mountain and excellent skiing in the winter.
✉ Lake Street just off the I-5 ☎ 530/926-3101

REDWOOD FOREST
☞☞☞☞ Benbow Inn ($$$)
Lakeside Tudor mansion built in 1926.
✉ 445 Lake Benbow Drive, Garberville ☎ 707/923-2124;
www.benbowinn.com ⊗ Closed Jan–Mar

SACRAMENTO
☞☞☞ Hyatt Regency ($$)
Conveniently located downtown, near the Capitol Building.
✉ 1209 "L" Street ☎ 916/443-1234

SANTA CRUZ

〜〜〜 Sea & Sand Inn ($$)

Budget hotel, overlooking the cliffs.

✉ 201 W Cliff Drive ☎ 831/427-3400; www.santacruzmotels.com

WINE COUNTRY

〜〜 〜〜 Fairmont Sonoma Mission Inn and Spa ($$$)

Exclusive spa in the Spanish-mission style.

✉ Sonoma Highway, Sonoma ☎ 707/938-9000; www.fairmont.com/sonoma

〜〜 〜〜 Foothill House Bed and Breakfast ($$$)

Charmingly remodeled, turn-of-the-20th-century farmhouse.

✉ 3037 Foothill Boulevard, Calistoga ☎ 707/942-6933

〜〜 〜〜 Harvest Inn ($$$)

Small English Tudor inn surrounded by vineyards. Many rooms have fireplaces and antique furnishings.

✉ One Main Street, St. Helena ☎ 707/963-9463; www.harvestinn.com

〜〜 Napa Inn ($$)

Romantic, turn-of-the-20th-century Victorian buildings comprise the Napa Inn. In downtown Napa near shops and restaurants.

✉ 1137 Warren Street, Napa ☎ 707/257-1444; www.napainn.com

〜〜 〜〜 Silverado Resort ($$$)

Large resort with wine tastings and sporting facilities.

✉ 1600 Atlas Peak Road, Napa ☎ 707/257-0200; www.silveradoresort.com

〜〜〜 Trojan Horse Inn ($$)

Very intimate. Only six rooms in this restored frontier home.

✉ 19455 Sonoma Highway, Sonoma ☎ 707/996-2430;
www.trojanhorseinn.com

YOSEMITE

〜〜 〜〜 Tenaya Lodge at Yosemite ($$)

Rustic elegance on the river, with cookouts and wagon rides.

✉ 1122 Highway 41 ☎ 559/683-6555

RESTAURANTS

EUREKA
♛♛♛ Sea Grill ($$)
Extensive seafood menu that includes cod Louisiana and Hawaiian mahi-mahi.
✉ 316 "E" St, Old Town ☎ 707/443-7187 🕐 Lunch, dinner. Closed Sun

MARIN COUNTY
Olema Farm House Restaurant ($$)
This shingle-sided eatery was a stagecoach stop in 1872, but today's fare is nouveau American.
✉ 10005 Highway 1, Olema ☎ 415/663-1264 🕐 Breakfast, lunch, dinner

MENDOCINO
♛♛ Mendocino Hotel Victorian Restaurant ($$$)
Cozy, antique-filled hotel. Dine in an elegant Victorian parlor or garden café. Excellent Continental cuisine and seafood specialties.
✉ 45080 Main Street ☎ 707/937-0511 🕐 Breakfast, lunch, dinner

WINE COUNTRY
Bistro Don Giovanni ($$$)
Serves Italian and Mediterranean specialties in a beautiful artistic setting. Daily pasta specials.
✉ 411 Howard Lane, Napa ☎ 707/224-3300 🕐 Lunch, dinner

♛♛♛♛ French Laundry ($$$)
Thomas Keller's famed new French restaurant takes reservations months in advance. Outdoor dining area. Prices are very steep.
✉ 6640 Washington Street, Yountville ☎ 707/944-2380 🕐 Lunch, dinner daily

Mustards ($$)
Napa Valley's trendiest and most popular spot for California cuisine. Reservations recommended.
✉ 7399 St Helena Highway, St. Helena ☎ 707/944-2424 🕐 Lunch, dinner

SHOPPING

ART AND ANTIQUES

Mendocino Arts Center
Two art galleries, along with numerous arts and crafts fairs.
✉ 45200 Little Lake Street, Mendocino ☎ 707/937-5818 and 800/653-3328

Railroad Square
A historic square featuring antiques stores, curio shops.
✉ Santa Rosa ☎ 707/578-8478

FACTORY OUTLETS

Folsom Factory Store
The 50 stores here include names like Nike, Jones NY, Bass.
✉ 13000 Folsom, Folsom

Mammoth Factory Store
Only 10 stores, but they are some of the best, with names like
Ralph Lauren, and Bass.
✉ 3343 Main Street, Mammoth Lakes

Outlets at Gilroy
More than 100 stores. Includes The Gap, Ann Taylor, Espirit among
others.
✉ 681 Leavesley, Gilroy

Petaluma Village Factory Outlet
Fifty stores from Saks to Coach to Gap.
✉ 2200 Petaluma Boulevard, Petaluma

GIFTS

All Seasons Cafe Wine Shop
A selection of the best of the hundreds of wine shops in Napa
Valley. Most sell gifts and other unique products, and will ship
anywhere in the world.
✉ 1400 Lincoln Avenue, Calistoga ☎ 707/942-9111

David Berkeley's
Eclectic variations from extensive wine selections by White House wine consultant, David Berkeley, to Epicurean European foods and country-flavored gifts.

✉ 515 Pavillions Lane, Sacramento ☎ 916/929-4422

Shaker Shops West
Quality reproductions of Shaker furniture and gifts, deep in California's north country.

✉ 5 Inverness Way, Inverness ☎ 415/669-7256

ENTERTAINMENT

NIGHTLIFE
Harlow's
Most glamorous nightclub in town. Upstairs is Momo's cigar lounge.

✉ 2708 "J" Street, Sacramento ☎ 916/441-4693

Lost Coast Brewery & Café
Microbreweries are the rage, and this is one of the best.

✉ 617 Fourth Street, Eureka ☎ 707/445-4480

Sacramento Brewing Company's Oasis
Locally produced, award-winning beer.

✉ 7811 Capitol Avenue, Sacramento ☎ 916/966-6274

SPORTS

Ski Lake Tahoe Association
Package deals available on the 15 downhill and 11 cross-country ski areas. Free shuttle between all.

☎ 888/824 6338 (Snow Ski); 530/544-7747 (Water Ski School), Lake Tahoe

Yosemite
Try rock-climbing, backpacking, camping, and hiking, guided or not. Sheer El Capitan mountain, at 3,500ft (1067m), attracts world-class climbers in search of a challenge.

Central Coast

The central coast is the least crowded, and features rolling hills meeting the quiet beach areas. There are plenty of parks in which to explore hiking and biking trails. Hearst Castle, which sits high above the shoreline, is an extraordinary architectural link to the California of another era. Morro Bay's beach area is perfect for a slower, more relaxed vacation.

Oxnard □

The diversity of the Central Coast is marked by the Danish-influenced town of Solvang. You can see thatched huts and real working windmills and enjoy any number of Scandinavian-style restaurants and shops. Further inland, the Santa Ynez valley boasts several wineries to rival any in the world.

Santa Barbara, Cambria and Montecito are all special in their own way, and should be on the itinerary of any visitor to California.

CARMEL

Carmel was established in the late 19th century and has since gained its reputation as a bohemian retreat. It has some of the most picturesque coastal residences in the state, many in Spanish-Mission style. **Mission San Carlos Borromeo del Rio Carmelo** (1769) was moved to its riverside site here in Carmel in 1771. Father Junípero Serra is buried in the church.

✚ 4K

Mission San Carlos Borromeo del Rio Carmelo

✉ 3080 Rio Road ☎ 831/624-1271 🕙 Mon–Fri 9:30–4:30, Sat, Sun 10:30–4:30 💷 Inexpensive

HEARST CASTLE

Best places to see, pages 44–45.

MONTEREY PENINSULA

Best places to see, pages 48–49.

MORRO BAY

Morro Rock, the conical, volcano-shaped rock that towers 578ft (176m) out of the Pacific Ocean, sits guarding the entrance to Morro Bay, which is known primarily for its commercial fishing and oyster farming. Although the town has a modest tourist trade, the locals are mostly concerned with the daily business of fishing. Beneath the rock stretches a 5-mile (8km) long beach with 85ft-

high (26m) white sand dunes that serve as a habitat for bird and plant life.

The Morro Bay Arts Festival takes place each weekend in October, and the **Museum of Natural History** exhibits marine life native to the central coast, including the Bay's entertaining sea lions. **Tiger's Folly Cruises** offers harbor cruises.

The State Park, south of Morro Bay, is beautiful and a must for those who enjoy camping and hiking. The campgrounds are at the southern end of the park surrounded by cypress and eucalyptus. The Galley Restaurant serves delicious seafood dishes.

✚ 5M ✉ 845 Embarcadero Road, Suite D ☎ 805/772-4467 🕐 Mon–Fri 8:30–5, Sat 10–4 ✋ Free

Museum of Natural History

✉ Morro Bay State Park ☎ 805/772-2694 🕐 Daily 10–5 ✋ Inexpensive

Tiger's Folly Cruises

✉ 1205 Embarcadero ☎ 805/772-2257 🕐 Call for times ✋ Inexpensive

OXNARD

Oxnard is a harbor town located on the Ventura–Los Angeles county line, and is home to an annual Strawberry Festival each May. Surpisingly overlooked by visitors are the 7 miles (11km) of beautiful beaches lining the town.

The **Carnegie Art Museum** has a permanent collection of 20th-century California painters, while changing exhibits feature photography and sculpture, with some shows spotlighting local artists. The **Ventura County Gull Wings Children's Museum's** hands-on exhibits of fossils and minerals, including a puppet theater and make-believe campground, will entertain the kids.

✚ 8W

Carnegie Art Museum

✉ 424 S "C" Street ☎ 805/385-8157 🕐 Thu–Sat 10–5, Sun 1–5 ✋ Inexpensive

Ventura County Gull Wings Children's Museum

✉ 418 W 4th Street ☎ 805/483-3005 🕐 Tue–Sat 10–5 ✋ Inexpensive

SALINAS

John Steinbeck was born in this working-class town 17 miles (27km) inland from Monterey, now home to the **National Steinbeck Center.** While it's sometimes overlooked in favor of its more affluent neighbors, Salinas is charming. For those visiting in August, there is the Steinbeck Festival. Many rodeo fans visit the town in July to catch one of the major stops on the professional rodeo circuit.

The Hat In Three Stages of Landing is a unique giant sculpture by Claes Oldenberg which captures a trio of bright yellow hats, each weighing 3,500lb (1,590kg). The sculpture graces the lawn of the Community Center, where there are art exhibits and musical/theatrical performances.

✚ 4K

National Steinbeck Center

✉ 1 Main Street ☎ 831/796-3833; www.steinbeck.org 🕐 Daily 10–5, closed major holidays ✋ Moderate

SANTA BARBARA

A pleasant and affordable day trip from Los Angeles by train (moderate cost) taking you along the Pacific coast in the morning, gives you time to explore the historic adobes and museums. Lunch on Stearns Wharf, explore the specialty shops there, then stroll the white-sand beach, or play a short round of golf before returning in late afternoon.

The County Courthouse, on Anacapa Street, is one of the best examples of Spanish-Moorish architecture in the US.

El Presidio de Santa Barbara State Historic Park, on the site of a late-1700 Spanish outpost, includes historical buildings such as El Cuartel, the second-oldest surviving edifice in California.

Mission Santa Barbara is the best preserved of the 21 California missions, and the church is filled with Mexican art from the 18th and 19th centuries. A Moorish fountain from 1808 graces the front and the mission is the site of The Little Fiesta each August.

The **Santa Barbara Museum of Art** has a wide variety of American, Asian and 19th-century French, Greek and Roman antiquities, including a major photographic collection.

Visit the Zoological Gardens which are natural habitats for 600 animals, and feature over 80 exhibits.

✚ 8W

El Presidio de Santa Barbara State Historic Park

✉ 122–129 E Canon Perdido Street ☎ 805/965-0093
🕐 Daily 10:30–4:30 💶 Free

Mission Santa Barbara

✉ E Los Olivos and Laguna Street ☎ 805/682-4149 🕐 Daily 9–5; closed major hols 💶 Inexpensive, under 16 free

Santa Barbara Museum of Art

✉ 1130 State Street ☎ 805/963-4364 🕐 Tue–Sun 10–4 💶 Moderate. Free Sun

SOLVANG

Denmark in California might best describe Solvang, with its Danish architecture, windmills, gaslights and cobblestone walks. A tour of Solvang is possible in a horse-drawn Danish streetcar, and the town hosts several remarkable festivals annually. Contrasting the Scandinavian motif is the 1804 **Old Mission Santa Ines.**

✚ 7V

Old Mission Santa Ines

✉ 1760 Mission Drive ☎ 805/688-4815 🕐 Summer 9–6, Oct–May 9–5:30; closed major holidays 💶 Inexpensive 🍴 Scandinavian restaurants or cafés ($–$$$)

ℹ Chamber of Commerce, 1693 Mission Drive ☎ 805/688-0701

VENTURA

This small beach town between Los Angeles and Santa Barbara is worth a brief visit.

San Buenaventura Mission was founded in 1782 by Father Junipero Serra and was reputed to be his favorite mission. The church is restored and the museum exhibits Native American artifacts from the Chumash tribes.

Next to the Mission is the Albinger Archaeological Museum. It displays over 3,500 years of remains, all from areas around the Mission, while Ventura County Museum of History and Art has Native American, Hispanic and pioneer exhibits.

🚼 8W

San Buenaventura Mission

✉ 211 East Main Street ☎ 805/643-4318 🕐 Mon–Fri 10–5, Sat 9–5, Sun 10–4; closed major holidays 🖐 Inexpensive

HOTELS

BIG SUR
⚜⚜⚜ Ventana Inn & Spa ($$$)
Luxurious hideaway, comprises 59 separate bungalows. Sweeping views of the coastline.

✉ California Highway 1 ☎ 831/667-2331; www.ventanainn.com

CARMEL
⚜⚜⚜ Sandpiper Inn by the Sea ($$)
Early California inn built in 1929. Some rooms with ocean views.

✉ 2408 Bay View Avenue ☎ 831/624-6433; www.sandpiper-inn.com

⚜⚜⚜⚜ Tickle Pink Inn ($$$)
Coastline views from secluded cottages and rooms. Nonchalant luxury. Afternoon wine and cheese service.

✉ 155 Highland Drive ☎ 831/624-1244; www.ticklepinkinn.com

HALF MOON BAY
⚜⚜⚜ The Beach House ($$$)
Large rooms with ocean views, fireplaces like an old New England summer home. Jacuzzis, saunas.

✉ 9 miles (14.5km) north of Half Moon Bay, 4100 Coast Highway 1
☎ 650/712-0220; www.beach-house.com

MONTEREY
⚜⚜⚜⚜ Old Monterey Inn ($$$)
English country hotel boasting acres of gardens and spectacular views of Monterey Bay.

✉ 500 Martin Street ☎ 831/375-8284; www.oldmontereyinn.com

RESTAURANTS

MONTECITO
⚜⚜⚜ Montecito Cafe ($$)
California cuisine; warm setting in The Montecito Inn.

✉ 1295 Coast Village Road ☎ 805/969-3392 🕐 Lunch, dinner

Stonehouse ($$$)

Regional cuisine in rustic, romantic setting. At the San Ysidro Ranch Resort.

✉ 900 San Ysidro Road ☎ 805/969-5046 ◷ Lunch, dinner

MORRO BAY

♦♦♦ Hoppe's Garden Bistro ($$)

International cuisine and great wine list.

✉ 78 North Ocean Avenue, Cayucos ☎ 805/772-9012 ◷ Lunch, dinner; closed Mon–Tue

OJAI

♦♦ Suzanne's Cuisine ($$)

A real gem off the beaten path. Inexpensive California cuisine.

✉ 502 W Ojai Avenue ☎ 805/ 640-1961 ◷ Lunch, dinner; closed Tue

SAN LUIS OBISPO

♦♦♦ Buona Tavola ($$)

A great-value Italian restaurant in a casual, country setting.

✉ 1037 Monterey Street ☎ 805/545-8000 ◷ Lunch Mon–Fri, dinner daily

SANTA BARBARA

♦♦ Brophy Brother's Clam Bar and Restaurant ($$)

Spectacular views and an energetic crowd.

✉ 119 Harbor Way ☎ 805/966-4418 ◷ Lunch, dinner

♦♦ Carlito's Cafe y Cantina ($)

Budget Mexican and interesting vegetarian plates.

✉ 1324 State Street ☎ 805/962-7117 ◷ Lunch, dinner

♦♦ The Hitching Post ($)

Barbecue, steaks and french fries in a casual roadhouse atmosphere.

✉ 406 E Highway 246, Buellton ☎ 805/688-0676

✉ 3325 Point Sal Road, Casmalia ☎ 805/937-6151 ◷ Dinner only

SHOPPING

FACTORY OUTLETS
American Tin Cannery Factory Outlet
Izod and Nine West are just two of the nearly 40 stores.

✉ 125 Ocean View Boulevard, Pacific Grove, Monterey

Pismo Beach Outlet Center
Jones New York, Bass, Mikasa, Levi's; 40 shops in all.

✉ 333 5-Cities Drive, Pismo Beach

Solvang Outlet Stores
Small but élite, featuring Donna Karen, Ellen Tracy, Brooks Bros.

✉ 3202 N Alisal Road, Solvang

GIFTS
Peter Rabbit and Friends
Toys, music boxes and clothing featuring some of the characters and scenes from Beatrix Potter's children's stories.

✉ Lincoln Avenue between 7th and Ocean avenues, Monterey Bay

☎ 831/624-6854

SPORTS

Mazda Raceway Laguna Seca
Four major auto races a year, including restored antique cars.

✉ 1021 Monterey Road, Salinas 93908 ☎ 831/648-5100

Monterey Bay Kayaks
Kayak rentals, tours.

✉ 693 Del Monte Avenue, Monterey ☎ 831/373-5357

Spyglass Hill
Less expensive than Pebble Beach course (which hosts the AT&T ProAm tour), the bordering Pacific and Del Monte Forest make this difficult but scenic. Reserve a month in advance (year for groups).

✉ Spyglass Hill Road, Pebble Beach ☎ 831/624-3811

Los Angeles

Los Angeles
□

Whether you come for the beaches, mountains, museums or movie stars, Los Angeles teems with activity. Bring your sunglasses and your tanning lotion because here in California there is plenty of sunshine. For dedicated sun-seekers, beautiful beaches stretch along the western edge of this seemingly endless metropolis. Zuma Beach is one of the best for enjoying the pastime made famous by the music of The Beach Boys – surfing.

At Venice Beach you can either stroll barefoot along the beach or join the hustle along the Boardwalk, where vendors hawk their souvenirs. This is home to some of the nation's most colorful characters: musicians, magicians and mime artists, as well as Muscle Beach body builders.

BEVERLY HILLS

The City of Stars is the place where shopping and the entertainment industry each vie for their place as the number one attraction (▶ 134–135). Here you will find some of the most expensive real estate in the country. The city's most recognizable zip code (90210) receives more than 14 million visitors a year, making it the most popular destination in Los Angeles.

Beverly Hills has several main thoroughfares, all running east to west. Sunset Boulevard, at the north end, roughly splits the commercial and residential areas. Wilshire Boulevard is the main thoroughfare to the business and commercial centers. At the south end, Pico Boulevard marks the Beverly Hills border.

www.lovebeverlyhills.org

✚ 9W

🛈 Visitors Bureau, 239 S Beverly Drive, Beverly Hills 90212

☎ 310/248-1015 🕓 Mon–Fri 8:30–5

CHINATOWN

The cultural center of this unique community is home to about 5 percent of LA's 200,000 Chinese residents. Chinatown encompasses 16 square blocks, and its downtown area is filled with Asian architecture, good restaurants and import shops. The Kong Chow Temple is exquisite.

✚ *Downtown LA 4c* ✉ 900 block of Broadway

CITY HALL

This was the first skyscraper to be built in Los Angeles and served as The Daily Planet Building in the *Superman* television series of the 1950s. Guided

tours are free (weekdays 10am–1pm) and last 45
minutes. There's an observation deck on the 27th floor.

✚ *Downtown LA 3e* ✉ 200 N Spring Street ☎ 213/978-0721
🕐 Mon–Fri 9–4 ✋ Free

DESCANSO GARDENS

These glorious gardens cover 65 acres (26ha), including a
30-acre (12ha) California live oak forest. Over 100,000
camellias from around the world flourish here, as do
many roses, lilacs and other blossoms. The Japanese
Garden has a serene teahouse, worth ta visit.

✚ 10W ✉ 1418 Descanso Drive, La Cañada Flintridge
☎ 818/949-4200 🕐 Daily 9–5. Closed Christmas Day
✋ Moderate, special discounts

EL PUEBLO DE LOS ANGELES STATE
HISTORICAL PARK

Here, on 44 acres (18ha) near downtown, you can visit
the Avila Adobe (the oldest adobe house), Masonic Hall,
Old Plaza Church and Sepulveda House. Founded in
1781, the main attraction for most visitors is Olvera
Street, an open-air Mexican-style market place lined with
specialty shops, vendors, cafés and restaurants.

✚ *Downtown LA 4d* ✉ Betweeen Alameda, Arcadia, Spring
and Macy streets ☎ 213/628-1274 🕐 Hours vary call for times
✋ Free

a walk around Beverly Hills

This walk begins on one of the most expensive shopping streets in the world.

Walk north from Wilshire on Rodeo Drive.

Do a spot of window-shopping in Tiffany's, Saks and other high end boutiques.

Proceed north several blocks to Little Santa Monica, then go east (right) a couple of blocks to Crescent.

On the corner of Crescent you'll see the historic former Beverly Hills Post Office and the magnificent Beverly Hills Municipal Building. The latter houses City Hall and the Beverly Hills library and police station.

Take a left on Crescent and proceed north across Santa Monica Boulevard and through the Beverly Hills "flatlands."

The homes along here are absolutely gorgeous.

At Sunset Boulevard, walk across to the newly restored Beverly Hills Hotel (➤ 144).

Take a few minutes to stroll through the splendid lobby.

Proceed east on Sunset to the West Hollywood business district.

Here you will pass the famous Roxy theater, Spago restaurant and The Whiskey A Go-Go.

Continue east, stopping for lunch at the chic Sunset Plaza, then on to Sunset. Turn right on Crescent Heights Road and go south to Melrose Avenue. Turn left on to Melrose and walk several blocks to Fairfax Avenue.

At this corner is the sprawling CBS Television City. Here you can get free tickets to live tapings of television shows.

South of CBS is the Farmers' Market and the Grove, where your tour ends.

Distance 4 miles (6.5km)
Time 3–4 hours, depending on time spent at attractions
Start point Beverly Hills, corner of Wilshire and Rodeo
End point Farmers' Market and the Grove complex of shops, restaurants and movie theaters
Lunch Chin Chin ($) ✉ 8618 Sunset Boulevard ☎ 310/652-1818

EXPOSITION PARK

The Los Angeles Memorial Coliseum was host to the Olympics in 1932 and 1984. Several museums are contained within, including the **California Museum of Science and Industry,** with interactive exhibits, Aerospace Complex and the surround-vision IMAX theater, featuring a five-story-high screen. Other museums include the **California Afro-American Museum** and the **Los Angeles County Museum of Natural History,** with three floors of dinosaur, fossil and cultural exhibits.

✚ *Downtown LA 1e (off map)*

California Museum of Science and Industry

✉ Exposition Boulevard at Figueroa ☎ 213/744-7400; www.californiasciencecenter.org ⊙ Daily 10–5 🖐 Free, charge for IMAX

California Afro-American Museum

✉ 600 State Drive, Exposition Park ☎ 213/744-7432 ⊙ Wed–Sat 10–4 🖐 Free ($6 parking fee)

LA County Museum of Natural History

✉ 900 Exposition Boulevard, Exposition Park ☎ 213/763-3466 ⊙ Mon–Fri 9:30–5, Sat, Sun 10–5 🖐 Moderate, free first Tue of month

FOREST LAWN MEMORIAL PARK

A cemetery may seem like an unusual attraction, but there are 300 lush acres (121ha) of grounds here, with reproductions of such works as da Vinci's *Last Supper*, and the world's largest religious painting on canvas, Jan Styke's *The Crucifixion*. Also not to be missed are the ornate tombstones of celebrities and the beautiful gardens. Forest Lawn cemetery is the final resting place of such Hollywood film legends as Humphrey Bogart, Errol Flynn, Spencer

STAN LAUREL
1890 – 1965
A MASTER OF COMEDY
HIS GENIUS IN THE ART OF
HUMOR BROUGHT GLADNESS
TO THE WORLD HE LOVED.

Tracy, Stan Laurel, Jean Harlow, Carole Lombard, W C Fields and Cary Grant.

✚ 9W ✉ 1712 South Glendale Avenue, Glendale ☎ 818/241-4151 ⊙ Daily 10–5 ✋ Free

GETTY CENTER

This billion-dollar arts complex sits high on a hill off the 405 San Diego freeway to the north of the city. Although still in its infancy it seems destined to become one of LA's main attractions. With everything from Greek sculptures to paintings by European masters and modern photography, the museum is surrounded by ponds, beautiful landscaping and a fine herb garden.

✚ 9W

Getty Center

✉ 1200 Getty Center Drive ☎ 310/440-7300 ⊙ Tue–Thu, Sun 10–6, Fri, Sat 10–9 ✋ Free ($7 fee for parking)

GRIFFITH PARK

Here, in the Santa Monica Mountain range, Griffith Park contains the LA Zoo, Griffith Observatory and Planetarium, as well as Travel Town, an outdoor transportation museum. The Observatory is the perfect spot to view the Hollywood sign and the entire city, while the Planetarium features incredible laserium shows. There are horseback riding and children's rides and attractions, plus plenty of picnic areas.

🚇 9W ✉ Mount Hollywood ☎ 323/664-1191 (Observatory/Planetarium); 323/666-4650 (Zoo); 323/913-4688 (tourist information) 🕔 Hours vary so call for information ✋ The park is free; some attractions have moderate fees

HOLLYWOOD
Best places to see, pages 46–47.

HOLLYWOOD WAX MUSEUM
Over 220 of Hollywood's greatest stars, political leaders and sports greats – all made of wax, but very lifelike – are on show at the Hollywood Wax Museum. Also included are displays on television, motion pictures and religion. Exhibits rotate every six months or so. The Chamber of Horrors is a favorite, as well as the recent additions of current stars.

🚇 9W (Hollywood) ✉ 6767 Hollywood Boulevard ☎ 323/462-8860 🕔 Sun–Thu 10–midnight, Fri–Sat to 1am ✋ Moderate

HUNTINGTON LIBRARY, ART GALLERY AND GARDENS
The historical library contains over four million items, including art treasures and an extraordinary treasury of rare and precious manuscripts. After taking in the Huntington's art and books, take a

walk through the immaculate botanical gardens, the best in the state. Here, 15 separate garden areas contain around 14,000 different types of plants and trees. Arrive early because the grounds fill up fast.

✚ 10W ✉ 1151 Oxford Road, San Marino ☎ 626/405-2141 🕐 Tue–Fri 12–4:30, Sat–Sun 10:30–4:30 👋 Moderate

LITTLE TOKYO

The city's Japanese quarter features the 40-shop Japanese Village Plaza, which resembles a rural village. Also here are Noguchi Plaza, with its fan-shaped Japan America Theater, the Japanese American National Museum, and quiet Japanese gardens. Some great sushi bars can also be found here.

✚ *Downtown LA 3f* ✉ First Street and Central Avenue

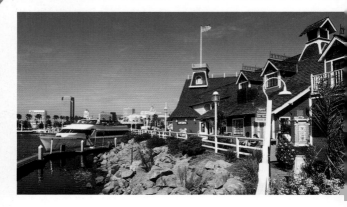

LONG BEACH

Long Beach is now California's fifth largest city. Its Shoreline Village and Wilmore Park surround the Convention and Entertainment Center, a popular corporate convention spot. Boats to Catalina Island depart from Golden Shore Boulevard. Of special interest is the *Queen Mary*, which came to rest in Long Beach in 1967. With 12 decks and weighing in at 50,000 tons, it is the largest passenger ship ever built, the *crème de la crème* of 1932 art deco luxury. There are lots of shops and eateries on board.

🚩 10X 🖂 Pier J, Long Beach Harbor ☎ 562/435-3511 🕐 Daily 10–5
👆 Free; moderate-priced guided tours

LOS ANGELES STATE AND COUNTY ARBORETUM

The trees and shrubs in the Los Angeles Arboretum are arranged according to the continent they originate from. Also featured are greenhouses, a bird sanctuary and historic buildings like the Queen Anne Cottage, home of the estate's former owner, Elia Jackson Baldwin. Picnic areas and tours available.

🚩 10W 🖂 301 N Baldwin Avenue, Arcadia ☎ 626/821-3222 🕐 Daily 9–4:30 👆 Inexpensive; various discounts

MANN'S CHINESE THEATRE

Originally Grauman's Chinese Theatre, Mann's, a prime Hollywood tourist attraction, is a good starting point for a tour of Los Angeles.

The theater was opened in 1927 by showman Sid Grauman, and whenever a film was premiered here, stars left their hand- or footprints.

🔶 9W (Hollywood) ✉ 6925 Hollywood Boulevard ☎ 323/464-8111

MUSEUM OF CONTEMPORARY ART (MOCA)

This seven-tiered museum (much of it below street level) has 11 giant pyramidal skylights and a 53ft (16m) barrel-vaulted entrance. It is dedicated to works of art since the 1940s and features traveling exhibitions. Also at Geffen Contemporary and Pacific Design Center.

🔶 *Downtown LA 2e* ✉ 250 S Grand Avenue ☎ 213/621-2766 🕐 Mon, Fri 11–5, Thu 11–8, Sat, Sun 11–6 ✋ Moderate; free Thu

PETERSEN AUTOMOTIVE MUSEUM

If you are an automotive fan, the Petersen Museum, with one of the largest auto collections in the world, is a must. It explores automotive history and culture from the earliest jalopies. Highlights are the 1957 Ferrari 250 Testa Rossa, and customized cars from Dean Jeffries and George Barris.

🔶 *Downtown LA 1c (off map)* ✉ 6060 Wilshire Boulevard ☎ 323/930-CARS 🕐 Tue–Sun 10–6 ✋ Moderate

SOUTHWEST MUSEUM
This mission-revival style building, high above downtown LA, focuses on Native American art, including jewelry, basketwork and weaving. The founder, Charles Lummis, director of the Los Angeles Library in 1907, also donated rare books to the museum.
➕ *Downtown LA 4b (off map)* ✉ 234 Museum Drive ☎ 323/221-2164
🕐 Tue–Sun 10–5 ✋ Moderate

UNIVERSAL STUDIOS AND CITYWALK
For a fascinating behind-the-scenes look at movie-making, plan to spend the better part of a day at Universal Studios, the world's biggest and busiest motion picture and television studio-cum-theme park. Citywalk features outdoor dining and a wide variety of shops that are a cut above what you might expect. There are huge outdoor screens that show music videos and movie previews and a theater complex shows all the latest movies.

The upper and lower sections are connected by a long escalator, making the 420-acre (170ha) park easy to navigate. Some of the more interesting sets still standing are from such films as *The Sting*, *Animal House* and *Home Alone*. There are theme rides based on other successful films such as *Revenge of the Mummy* and *Jurassic Park*.
www.universalstudios.com; **www.**citywalk.com
➕ 9W (Hollywood) ✉ 100 Universal City Plaza, Universal City ☎ 800-UNIVERSAL 🕐 Daily from 9 or 10am; closing hours vary ✋ Expensive

VENICE BEACH

Just south along the beach from Santa Monica is Venice Beach. Although it appears to be a throwback to the 1960s, it is really a thriving enclave for modern bohemians. The neighborhood was founded in 1905 by Abbot Kinney, who hoped to create a haven for artistic types. Gondolas were imported from Italy and, for a time, the canals were eerily similar to those in Europe. Try a free self-guided tour. The most popular today is the Ocean Front Walk, teeming with visitors, street performers and souvenir stands. You can also rent a bicycle or rollerblades.

✚ 9W ✉ 15 miles (24km) from downtown Los Angeles, access via Lincoln Boulevard

WATTS TOWERS AND ARTS CENTER

Italian immigrant Simon Rodia took 30 years to build these extraordinary towers by himself, using scraps of whatever materials he could find. The Arts Center, next to the towers, contains rotating exhibits of African American art.

✚ 9W ✉ 1765 E 107th Street ☎ 213/847-4646 🕐 Tower Tours: Fri–Sun 11–4 ✋ Inexpensive

Arts Center

✉ 1727 107th Street 🕐 Tue–Sat 10–4, Sun 12–4 ✋ Inexpensive

HOTELS

Bel Age ($$$)
All-suite hotel in the heart of West Hollywood. Rooftop swimming pool with fantastic views of the city.
✉ 1020 N San Vicente Boulevard ☎ 310/854-1111; www.belage.com

▼▼ ▼▼ Beverly Hills Hotel ($$$)
A 1912 landmark restored in the early 1990s by its owner, the Sultan of Brunei. Famous for its private bungalows and the celebrity-packed Polo Lounge.
✉ 9641 Sunset Boulevard ☎ 310/276-2251; www.thebeverlyhillshotel.com

Chateau Marmont Hotel ($$$)
Favorite of film and music communities in the style of a Loire Valley château.
✉ 8221 Sunset Boulevard ☎ 323/656-1010; www.chateaumarmont.com

▼▼▼ Hollywood Roosevelt ($$)
Site of first Academy Awards presentation (1927). Centrally located (➤ 46.
✉ 7000 Hollywood Boulevard ☎ 323/466-7000; www.hollywoodroosevelt.com

▼▼▼ Hotel Bel-Air ($$$)
Most exotic of all LA hotels with a Mediterranean feel. A favorite hideaway for the rich and famous.
✉ 701 Stone Canyon Road ☎ 310/472-1211; www.hotelbelair.com

▼▼▼ Malibu Beach Inn ($$$)
Mediterranean-style hotel on a white-sand shore.
✉ 22878 Pacific Coast Highway, Malibu ☎ 310/456-6444; www.malibubeachinn.com

▼▼▼ New Otani Hotel ($$$)
Japanese-style hotel in the Little Tokyo area of downtown LA. Beautiful gardens and well-appointed rooms.
✉ 120 S Los Angeles Street ☎ 213/629-1200; www.newotani.com

▼▼▼ Sheraton Universal ($$$)

Views of Hollywood Hills and San Fernando Valley. Close to
Universal City attractions. Good-value weekend packages.

✉ 333 Universal Hollywood Drive Parkway ☎ 818/980-1212

Shutters on the Beach ($$$)

Contemporary beachfront hotel with all the amenities. Marble
bathrooms, sweeping ocean views.

✉ 1 Pico Boulevard, Santa Monica ☎ 310/458-0030;
www.shuttersonthebeach.com

Sofitel Los Angeles ($$)

Mediterranean-style hotel with affordable rates. Across from the
Beverly Center mall (► 150).

✉ 8555 Beverly Boulevard ☎ 310/278-5444; www.sofitella.com

Sunset Marquis ($$$)

Mediterranean décor, mostly suites. It's a favorite of the
entertainment community for its casual, comfortable atmosphere.

✉ 1200 N Alta Loma Road ☎ 310/657-1333; www.sunsetmarquishotel.com

Sunset Tower Hotel ($$$)

An LA landmark; 15 stories of art deco elegance at the end of
Sunset Strip. Popular movie location.

✉ 8358 Sunset Boulevard, W Hollywood ☎ 323/654-7100;
www.sunsettowerhotel.com

RESTAURANTS

Apple Pan ($)

A throwback to the 1940s (authentic) this LA institution serves
fresh, juicy hamburgers, tasty fries and pie at a burger counter.

✉ 10801 W Pico Boulevard ☎ 310/475-3585 🕐 Lunch, dinner; closed Mon

Border Grill ($$)

Hip cantina by the beach. Serves exotic Mexican specialties.
Stylish ambience; great margaritas.

✉ 1445 4th Street, Santa Monica ☎ 310/451-1655 🕐 Lunch, dinner

Buffalo Club ($$$)

Westside club/restaurant, with top-notch American cuisine.

✉ 1520 Olympic Boulevard (at 15th Street) ☎ 310/450-8600 🕐 Lunch, dinner

Cheesecake Factory ($)

One of the most popular restaurants in Southern California because of its huge portions of traditional American fare and a gauntlet of cheesecake.

✉ 364 N Beverly Drive, Beverly Hills ☎ 310/278-7270
✉ 4142 Via Marina, Marina del Rey ☎ 310/306-3344 🕐 Lunch, dinner

♦♦ Dan Tana's ($$$)

Long-time celebrity hangout for Italian food, the best steaks and fresh lobster. Very Hollywood.

✉ 9071 Santa Monica Boulevard ☎ 310/275-9444 🕐 Dinner only, but open late

Duke's ($)

Sunset Strip coffee shop/ diner where fantastic omelettes attract the young and hip. Long lines at breakfast, especially on weekends.

✉ 8909 Sunset Boulevard ☎ 310/652-3100 🕐 Breakfast, lunch, dinner

♦♦ El Cholo ($$)

Long-established family-owned Mexican serving traditional fare since 1927. Another location is in Santa Monica.

✉ 1121 S Western Avenue ☎ 323/734-2773 🕐 Lunch, dinner

♦♦♦ The Ivy ($$$)

Great American food and the place to see and be seen in LA. Outdoor patio. Reservations are a must.

✉ 113 N Robertson Boulevard ☎ 310/274-8303 🕐 Lunch, dinner

♦♦♦ Lawry's Prime Rib ($$$)

The best for prime rib anywhere, supposedly, in the world. "To die for," says one. You decide, but make reservations early.

✉ 100 N La Cienega ☎ 866/223-8224 🕐 Dinner only

▼▼▼ Matsuhisa ($$$)

The flagship restaurant of the growing Nobu empire, Matsuhisa serves fresh and fantastic sushi and sashimi in a bustling, slightly cramped setting.

✉ 129 N La Cienega ☎ 310/659-9639 🕐 Lunch Mon–Fri, dinner daily

Matteo's ($$$)

A one-time Rat Pack hang-out, with roomy leather booths and crimson walls, Matteo's has been serving traditional Italian food since 1963. Great for celebrity-watching.

✉ 2321 Westwood Boulevard ☎ 310/475-4521 🕐 Dinner Tue–Sun

▼▼ Musso & Frank Grill ($$)

A touch of "Old Hollywood" serving traditional fare. Great martinis and the best Caesar salad in LA.

✉ 6667 Hollywood Boulevard ☎ 323/467-7788 🕐 Lunch, dinner; closed Sun, Mon

▼▼▼ L'Orangerie ($$$)

Excellent modern-classic French food that is second only to the impressive décor. Impeccable service; terrace dining. Consistently in California's top listings. Dress code.

✉ 903 N La Cienega Boulevard ☎ 310/652-9770 🕐 Dinner only; closed Sun, Mon

▼▼▼ Pacific Dining Car ($$$)

Downtown standard for steaks and seafood. Draws daytime business crowd but is best in the evening. Reservations recommended.

✉ 1310 W 6th Street ☎ 213/483-6000 🕐 Breakfast, lunch, dinner

▼▼▼ Parkway Grill ($$)

The continental cuisine is worth the trip to Pasadena. Also California fare.

✉ 510 S Arroyo Parkway, Pasadena ☎ 626/795-1001 🕐 Lunch Mon–Fri, dinner daily

⬦⬦ ⬦⬦ Patina ($$$)
Comfortable and unpretentious French bistro.
✉ 141 S Grand Avenue ☎ 213/972-3331 🕐 Lunch, dinner

Roscoe's House of Chicken and Waffles ($)
Famous with locals for its informal setting, sinfully greasy chicken and delectable waffles any time of day. Several locations.
✉ 1514 N Gower Street (at Sunset Boulevard) ☎ 323/466-7453
🕐 Breakfast, lunch, dinner, open late

⬦⬦⬦ Spago ($$$)
World-renowned for chef Wolfgang Puck's gourmet pizzas, and its star-studded Academy Awards party. Also fine California cuisine.
✉ 176 N Canon Drive ☎ 310/385-0880 🕐 Dinner only

⬦⬦ Surya India ($$)
Samosas, tandoori and curries near the farmers' market.
✉ 8048 W 3rd Street ☎ 323/653-5151 🕐 Lunch, dinner

Tommy's Original Hamburger ($)
Perhaps the greatest hamburger stand on the planet. Greasy, but great!
✉ 2575 Beverly Boulevard ☎ 213/389-9060 🕐 Daily 24hrs; no credit cards

Trattoria Farfalla ($)
Italian café serving great thin-crust pizzas. Usually crowded, but worth the wait.
✉ 1978 N Hillhurst Street, Los Feliz ☎ 323/661-7365 🕐 Lunch, dinner

⬦⬦ ⬦⬦ Valentino ($$$)
Elegant, expensive Italian, with a great wine list and impeccable service. Reservations required.
✉ 3115 Pico Boulevard, Santa Monica ☎ 310/829-4313 🕐 Dinner; lunch only on Fri; closed Sun

SHOPPING

ART AND ANTIQUES

La Cienega Boulevard south of Santa Monica Boulevard, Beverly Boulevard west of the Beverly Center, Melrose Avenue in Hollywood, and Santa Monica's Third Street Promenade are all lined with excellent, but costly antiques stores and art galleries.

CRAFTS
Olvera Street

Mexican crafts and gifts, clothing and cafés on LA's oldest street.
✉ Los Angeles Street

FASHION
Garment District

Fashion bargains in open store fronts and inside the huge Cooper Building. Stroll through the California Mart to see upcoming fashions.
✉ Los Angeles Street and 7th Street, Downtown

Melrose Avenue

See page 62.

Rodeo Drive

See page 62.

Venice Beach

Unique and amazingly inexpensive sunwear and hip formal dress.
✉ Oceanfront Walk, Venice

GIFTS
Hollywood Boulevard

The place to go to find rare movie memorabilia and posters. Theaters and restaurants for every mood and budget.
✉ Between La Brea and Highland

Little Tokyo

Unusual Oriental items. Outdoor shopping/dining.

✉ San Pedro and First streets, Downtown

Venice Beach

Outdoor booths with great prices, if you aren't distracted by the street artists and Muscle Beach iron-pumpers.

✉ Oceanfront between Washington and Santa Monica boulevards

FARMERS MARKET

Over 100 sellers of not only fresh produce but gifts, food and clothes, all at affordable prices. Open-air cafés.

✉ Third and Fairfax, Hollywood

STORES

Beverly Center

Three-tiered upscale mall, with exterior elevators that offer a great view of the area. Macy's, Broadway, Bullocks, Hard Rock Café.

✉ Beverly Boulevard and La Cienega, Beverly Hills

Westside Pavilion

Multi-level with modern, open-air atrium; Nordstrom, Robinsons-May and others.

✉ Pico and Westwood boulevards

ENTERTAINMENT

CONCERT HALLS

Hollywood Bowl

Outdoor arena, year-round headline concerts of every music style, especially the LA Philharmonic.

✉ 2301 N Highland Avenue, Hollywood ☎ 323/850-2000

Wiltern Theatre

Intimate, acoustically wonderful hall that features top-name musical performances in the art deco Wiltern Center.

✉ Wilshire and Western ☎ 213/480-3232

NIGHTLIFE

Bar Marmont

Intimate French colonial café, usually full of celebrities and paparazzi.

✉ 6171 Sunset Boulevard, Hollywood ☎ 323/650-0575

BB King's Blues Club

Three floors. Lucille's room is acoustic on Fri and Sat.

✉ 1000 Universal City Drive, Universal City ☎ 818/622-5464

Cat & Fiddle Pub and Restaurant

Ambient outdoor patio. Sunday jazz jam. No cover.

✉ 6530 Sunset Boulevard, Hollywood ☎ 323/468-3800

Cowboy Palace Saloon

The last real honky tonk in California. Live country seven nights. Pool, darts, dance classes. No cover.

✉ 21635 Devonshire Street, Chatsworth ☎ 818/341-0166

Good Luck Bar

Knocked out of the No. 1 spot by Bar Marmont, but now you finally have room to dance and enjoy yourself.

✉ 1514 Hillhurst Avenue, Los Feliz ☎ 323/666-3524

The Improvisation (Improv)

See the place where many comedians got their start.

✉ 8162 Melrose, West Hollywood ☎ 323/651-2583

The Mint

Live jazz, blues and R&B in this small club. Top artists often play here.

✉ 6010 Pico Boulevard ☎ 323/954-9400

Molly Malone's Irish Pub

Small neighborhood bar with Irish folk, rock & roll, R & B nightly. Cover varies.

✉ 575 S Fairfax ☎ 323/935-1577

Rage
Gay/lesbian meeting place, alternative/underground music.
✉ 8911 Santa Monica Boulevard, West Hollywood ☎ 310/652-7055

PERFORMING ARTS
Music Center of Los Angeles County
Includes Dorothy Chandler Pavilion, Mark Taper Forum, featuring experiment plays; the Ahmanson, with musical comedies and the Walt Disney Concert Hall.
✉ 135 N Grand, downtown ☎ 213/972-7211

SPORTS

Los Angeles Galaxy
The Los Angeles soccer team play at the Home Depot Center.
✉ 18400 Avalon Boulevard, Carson ☎ 310/630-2200

Moonlight Rollerway
Moonlight is one of the more popular indoor roller-blading rinks in LA.
✉ 5110 San Fernando Road, Glendale ☎ 818/241-3630

Pershing Square
The outdoor ice rink opens in November.
✉ Pershing Square Station on Metro Red Line ☎ 818/243-6488

Santa Anita Race Track
Bet on horses during the track's season, from December to April.
✉ 285 West Huntington Drive ☎ 626/574-7223 🕙 Dec 26–late Apr

Sports Center Bowl
The landmark Jerry's Deli is right next door for a snack, after you've worked up an appetite.
✉ 12655 Ventura Boulevard, Studio City ☎ 818/769-7600 🕙 Call for open bowling hours

Southern California

The commercial center of the state, Southern California is the most densley populated area. The vast metropolitan areas of Los Angeles and San Diego are surrounded by largely empty deserts.

San Diego

Southern California is also the center of the entertainment and aerospace industries. Hollywood, Disneyland and the many beaches that stretch south to Mexico are the favorites of most people who visit the area. There is a distinct Spanish influence in the architecture, and most of the missions are located along the coast between San Diego and Los Angeles.

ANAHEIM

Anaheim was originally founded as the center of a wine-producing colony by German immigrants in 1857. The vineyards were replaced by orange groves late in the 19th century, after a brutal drought. Oranges thrived until the 1950s, when commercial interests and the rapid growth of the Los Angeles metropolitan area took over. The two main attractions in the area are Disneyland Park (► 40–41) and Knott's Berry Farm (► 160).

🔒 10X ✉ 46 miles (74km) from Los Angeles via I–5; directly across from Disneyland

BAKERSFIELD

Bakersfield is California's main oil-producing center. Many consider it a less-than-desirable part of California, its furnace-like, 100°F-plus (38°C) summers a major drawback. However, the downtown area is a mix of restored buildings and newer offices. Of note are a genuine schoolhouse, church and a fully restored 1868 log cabin.

The **California Living Museum** focuses on the state's wildlife and native plants, many of which are rare or endangered.

Kern County Museum has exhibits representing both the human and the natural history of the area.

➕ 9U

California Living Museum
✉ 10500 Alfred Harrell Highway ☎ 661/872-2256 🕐 Daily 9–5 🍴 Picnic facilities ✋ Inexpensive

Kern County Museum
✉ 3801 Chester Avenue ☎ 661/852-5000 🕐 Mon–Sat 10–5, Sun noon–5 ✋ Inexpensive

BARSTOW

Barstow is the halfway point between Los Angeles and Las Vegas. It was settled in the early 19th century when silver mines flourished in the surrounding areas. The town of **Calico** boomed in the late 1800s, and its mines produced $15 million worth of ore. When the price of silver dropped, the town went bust. Today, you can visit the "ghost town" of Calico to pan for gold, ride the steam railway or see a show at the Calikage Playhouse.

North of Barstow is **Rainbow Basin National Natural Landmark.** Fossils, the forces of nature and an abundance of minerals give it its dramatic shapes and colors.

➕ 11V

Calico Ghost Town
✉ 11 miles (18km) northeast of Barstow via I-15 ☎ 760/254-2122 🕐 Daily 9–5 🍴 Restaurants moderate ✋ Inexpensive

Rainbow Basin National Natural Landmark
✉ Fossil Bed Road, 8 miles (13km) north of Barstow via SR 58

BIG BEAR LAKE

One of California's largest recreation areas, the Big Bear Lake region has two distinct sections; Big Bear Lake and Big Bear City, on the eastern end of the lake. Big Bear Village, centered around the lake, is popular for lodging, dining and shopping. Camping, hiking and riding are available in summer and skiing in winter.

➕ 11W ✉ Big Bear Chamber of Commerce, 630 Bartlett Road ☎ 909/866-4607; www.bigbearchamber.com 🍴 Many restaurants ($–$$$)

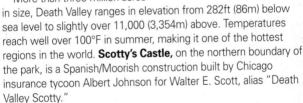

CATALINA ISLAND

Best places to see, pages 38–39.

DEATH VALLEY NATIONAL PARK

Three million years ago, inner-earth forces tormented, twisted and shook the land in what is now Death Valley, creating snowcapped mountains and superheated valleys. Lakes, formed during the Ice Age, evaporated, leaving alternating layers of mud and salt deposits.

More than three million acres in size, Death Valley ranges in elevation from 282ft (86m) below sea level to slightly over 11,000 (3,354m) above. Temperatures reach well over 100°F in summer, making it one of the hottest regions in the world. **Scotty's Castle,** on the northern boundary of the park, is a Spanish/Moorish construction built by Chicago insurance tycoon Albert Johnson for Walter E. Scott, alias "Death Valley Scotty."

➕ 11S 🖂 Furnace Creek Visitors Center ☎ 760/786-3244 🕧 Daily 8–5 🖐 Inexpensive ❓ Camping facilities

Scotty's Castle
☎ 760/786 2392 🕧 Daily 8–5 🖐 Moderate

FRESNO

Fresno lies in the heart of the San Joaquin Valley. One of the foremost agricultural areas in the country, it is also the gateway to the Sierra Nevada's three national parks.

The town's fine **Metropolitan Museum of Art, History and Science** features an extensive collection of Asian art, as well as American still-life paintings. Wild Water Adventure Park, on E Shaw

Avenue, contains over 20 water rides, pools and a
small fishing lake.

✚ 8S

Metropolitan Museum of Art, History and Science

✉ 1555 Van Ness Avenue ☎ 559/441-1444 ⏱ Tue–Sun 11–5
✋ Inexpensive

JOSHUA TREE NATIONAL MONUMENT

Known for its distinctive Joshua trees (a desert tree of
the yucca species), and its uniquely shaped rock
formations, the park connects the "high" and "low"
deserts. In the park is Key's View, a high elevation with
incredible views on a clear day. Not to be missed is
the Cholla Cactus Garden, about 10 miles (16km)
south of the Oasis Visitors Center.

✚ 12X ✉ Oasis Vistors Center, National Monument Drive, 29 Palms
☎ 760/367-5500 ⏱ Daily 8–5 ✋ Inexpensive

LAKE ARROWHEAD

Known locally as a sophisticated mountain getaway, this is where LA's wealthy spend leisurely weekends in luxury homes. Restrictive development laws help preserve the area's natural beauty. Swimming and boating are popular activities in summer, and skiing in winter. Children will enjoy the **Lake Arrowhead Children's Museum,** which contains historical information on the area and anthropological exhibitions.

www.lakearrowhead.net

➕ 11W

🛈 Chamber of Commerce, Lake Arrowhead Village ☎ 909/337-3715

🕐 Mon–Fri 9–5, Sat 10–3

Lake Arrowhead Children's Museum

✉ Lake Arrowhead Village ☎ 909/336-3093 🕐 Daily 10–5, 10–6 in summer

✋ Inexpensive

ORANGE COUNTY

Known by Californians as the "conservative" enclave of the state, Orange County is a sprawling expanse of humanity between Los Angeles and San Diego, with its own unique charms.

Disneyland Park

Best places to see, pages 40–41.

Festival of the Arts/Pageant of the Masters

A state-of-the-art art exhibit in the scenic wooded Laguna Canyon, this is a landmark event, the former featuring an exhibit of 150 Laguna artists of all kinds. The most interesting aspect of this seven-week event, however, is the Pageant of the Masters, in which human models stand perfectly still for three minutes in re-creations of famous paintings and sculptures, with a musical accompaniment.

✛ 10X ✉ Laguna Canyon Road, Laguna Beach ☎ 949/494-1145
🕓 Jul–Aug 10am–11pm 🖐 Expensive

Huntington Art Center

Though small, the Huntington Art Center is concerned with local contemporary art and architecture in a big way. It has been renovated and is a favorite with many local artists. Films are shown the first and third Friday of each month.

✛ 10X ✉ 538 Main Street E, Huntington Beach ☎ 714/374-1650
🕓 Wed–Sun noon–6, Sun noon–4 🖐 Free

International Surfing Museum

Huntington Beach calls itself "Surf City," with good reason, and is a mecca for surfing enthusiasts. Exhibits tell the sport's history, and the store sells surf gear, all, of course, to the music of the Beach Boys.

✛ 10X ✉ Olive Street, block off Main, Huntington Beach ☎ 714/960-3483
🕓 Summer daily noon–5; winter Thu–Mon noon–5 🖐 Inexpensive

Knott's Berry Farm

One of California's original theme parks, Knott's has grown from a true berry farm to a modern 150-acre (61-ha) attraction with over 165 rides. The Western theme areas include Ghost Town and Gold Mine Ride. Other attractions include Camp Snoopy, Wild Water Wilderness, Mystery Lodge, Reflection Lake, California Marketplace and Kingdom of the Dinosaurs. For the adventurous, there are four awesome rollercoasters, the Boomerang, Montezooma's Revenge, the Jaguar and the Silver Bullet. And, finally, for the truly hungry, Knott's serves its original, delicious, world-famous boysenberry pie.

✚ 10X ✉ 8039 Beach Boulevard, Buena Park ☎ 714/220-5200 ⏰ Subject to change; call for current times ✋ Expensive

Laguna Art Museum

The Laguna Art Museum was founded in 1918 and is the showcase venue for the Laguna Art Association. It usually features several visiting exhibits of paintings and sculpture by California artists. On permanent display are historical California landscapes and vintage photographs of the region.

✚ 10X ✉ Pacific Coast Highway and Cliff Drive, Laguna Beach ☎ 949/494-8971 ⏰ Daily 11–5 ✋ Moderate

Mission San Juan Capistrano

Founded in 1776, this is one of California's most beautiful missions, and the only building still standing where Father Junípero Serra said Mass. On 19 March each year, the Feast of St. Joseph celebrates the legendary "return of the swallows."

✚ 10X ✉ Corner of Ortega Highway/Camino Capistrano ☎ 949/234-1300
🕐 Daily 8:30–5

Sherman Library and Gardens

The unique gardens here are filled with orchids and koi ponds, while the library itself is a large building, taking up a whole city block. It functions as a center of historical research for the region. There is an extensive collection of historical Orange County documents and photographs.

✚ 10X ✉ 2647 E Coast Highway, Newport Beach ☎ 949/673-2261
🕐 Gardens daily 10:30–4 ✋ Inexpensive

Yorba Linda

The **Richard Nixon Presidential Library and Birthplace**, in Yorba Linda, has galleries, theaters and gardens, and personal memorabilia of this former US president. The grounds feature the small house where he was born, his post-presidency private study and a re-creation of the White House's Lincoln Sitting Room.

✚ 10X ✉ 18001 Yorba Linda Boulevard ☎ 714/993-3393;
www.nixonlibrary.org 🕐 Mon–Sat 10–5, Sun 11–5 ✋ Moderate

PALM SPRINGS

Rising out of the desert like an oasis, Palm Springs is one of the most famous resort towns in the world. It has become a favorite of wealthy retirees with a penchant for good golf and bad driving habits, and an ever-increasing number of young people are looking here for a brief spring retreat from their studies. The summers are insufferably hot, however, and the population dwindles from June through early September.

Anza-Borrego Desert State Park offers spectacular desert scenery. Set in 600,000 acres (242,915ha), the main flora includes lupin, poppy, dune primrose, desert sunflower and desert lily. A variety of short trails and camp-grounds can be found here.

Five miles (8km) south of Palm Springs is **Agua Caliente Indian Reservation.** The Tribal Council here has opened part of the reservation for hiking and picnics.

An awesome view of the San Jacinto Mountains awaits if you ride the **Palm Springs Aerial Tramway,** almost 5,000ft (1,524m) straight up. The perfect way to escape the debilitating summer heat, you ride up to the wooded trails and campgrounds at the top, where refreshments are available.

➕ 11X

Anza-Borrego Desert State Park

✉ Visitors Center, 2 miles (3.2km) west of Borrego Springs Township

☎ 760/767-4205;

www.anzaborregostatepark.org 🕐 Call for hours and more information

✋ Inexpensive

Agua Caliente Indian Reservation

☎ 760/323-0151 🕐 Wed–Sat 10–5, Sun noon–5 (shorter hours in summer)

✋ Inexpensive

Palm Springs Aerial Tramway

✉ Tramway Road, 3 miles (5km) southwest of SR 111
☎ 760/325-1391 🕐 Mon–Fri 10–8, Sat–Sun 8–8.
Closed 2 weeks in Aug ✋ Expensive

PALOMAR MOUNTAIN

Palomar Observatory houses the world-famous
200in (513cm) Hale telescope. High above the
distracting, bright city lights, the observatory also
has several smaller telescopes, used to monitor
the planet's movement. The small Greenway
Museum contains photographs of the
observatory's celestial sightings.

✚ 11Y ✉ 40 miles (65km) northeast of San Diego on
SR 6 ☎ 626/395-4033 🕐 Daily 9–4 ✋ Free

RIVERSIDE

Because the region has the ideal climate and
soil for growing navel oranges, this was the wealthiest US city per
capita and the metropolitan center of Southern California at the
turn of the 20th century. Several buildings remain from around this
time: the Italian Renaissance-style City Hall, the Classic Revival
municipal museum, and many exquisite Victorian homes. In
addition, mission architecture and adobe residences still reflect
the early wealth and prestige.

California Citrus State Historic Park features a grove of 80
varieties of citrus trees. The visitor center is located in a Victorian
house. The Riverside Municipal Museum, at 3720 Orange Street,
traces the history of citrus-growing in the region.

✚ 10W

California Citrus State Historic Park

✉ Van Buren Boulevard at Dufferin Avenue ☎ 951/780-6222 🕐 Daily 8–5
(until 7 Apr–Sep); visitor center Wed, Sat, Sun 10–4 ✋ Free 🍴 Picnic
facilities

SAN DIEGO

San Diego rarely gets rain, never freezes, has an average annual daytime temperature between 58 and 70°F (14 and 21°C), and more than 70 miles (113km) of sandy beaches. California's second largest city, it retains a small-town ambience. Ralph Waldo Emerson must have visited San Diego when he said "California has better days and more of them."

✚ 11Z

Balboa Park

Best places to see, pages 36–37.

The Beaches

The most popular of the city's beaches is Pacific Beach (known as "PB" by the locals), which features The Tourmaline Surfing Park, a surfer's paradise. Mission Beach has a 3-mile (5km) walk of shops and skateboard, rollerblade and bicycle rental stands. Ocean Beach is one of the liveliest in San Diego, and a good place to fish. Point Loma is an upscale beach, with spectacular views of the naval ships' comings and goings.

Cabrillo National Monument

A 144-acre (58ha) park along steep cliffs, Cabrillo rewards with great views of San Diego Bay, and it's an especially good place to spot gray whales migrating to Mexico between mid-December and mid-March. The Old Point Loma Lighthouse, dating from 1855, is 25 miles (43km) out to sea, but visible from here on a clear day.

✉ 10 miles (16km) west of I-8 on Catalina Boulevard ☎ 619/557-5450
🕐 Daily 9–5:15 👋 Inexpensive

Coronado Island

A combination of wealthy enclave and naval base, Coronado sits just across the bay from downtown San Diego. The easiest way to reach it is on the Bay Ferry. Leaving from Broadway Pier downtown, the ferry arrives at Old Ferry Landing in Coronado in 15 minutes. You can also reach the island via the towering San Diego–Coronado Bay Bridge (toll). The main attraction on the island is Hotel Del Coronado (➤ 179). A testament to the beauty of Victorian architecture, the "Del" was opened in 1888, and film buffs might remember it as one of the main locations in Marilyn Monroe's film *Some Like It Hot.*

✉ Visitor Center at 1100 Orange Avenue ☎ 619/236-1212 ☎ 619/437-8788 (Visitor Center), 619/234-4111 (Bay Ferry information) ✋ Inexpensive

Gaslamp Quarter
The reclamation of San Diego's 19th-century Gaslamp Quarter is one of urban America's great success stories. Slated for demolition, many of its Victorian-era cast-iron and other buildings were restored and converted into stores, restaurants and nightclubs, and the area is now the center of San Diego's vibrant nightlife.
www.gaslamp.org

House of Pacific Relations

The culture and art of 31 nations is housed in the museum's 15 California/Spanish-style cottages located in the Pan American Plaza. Other Plaza attractions are the Aerospace Museum, San Diego Automotive Museum and the open-air Starlight Bowl.

✉ 2125 Park Boulevard, Balboa Park ☎ 619/234-0739 ⏰ Sun, 2nd and 4th Tue of month ✋ Free; donations welcome

La Jolla

Pronounced *La Hoya* (Spanish for "The Jewel"), this picturesque cove, just north of San Diego, is one of the prettiest places in the whole state. This unspoiled piece of coastline offers expensive restaurants and boutiques on its two main thoroughfares: Prospect Street and Girard Avenue. Just north of La Jolla are the equally scenic towns of Del Mar and Solana Beach. Relatively undiscovered by tourists, these beaches epitomize the beauty and tranquillity of Southern California.

✉ 10 miles (16km) north of San Diego via I 805 or Highway 1

Maritime Museum of San Diego

Just three ships are moored on the Embarcadero but oh, what legendary ships they are! The pick of the bunch is the 1863 *Star of India*, a fully equipped three-mast sailing ship, the oldest iron-hulled ship in America still afloat. San Francisco's *Berkeley* was the ferry used to evacuate victims of the 1906 earthquake. The 1904 steam-powered yacht *Medea* occasionally sails around the Bay.

✉ 1492 North Harbor Drive ☎ 619/234-9153 🕐 Daily 9–8 (closes 9pm in summer) 🖐 Moderate

Mission Bay Park

There are miles of cycling paths throughout this huge aquatic park, and a bicycle rental stand can be found just off East Mission Bay Drive. Kite flying and volleyball are popular pastimes here, and watersports, as well as golf, picnicking and camping, can be found. The park is also the home of Sea World (➤ 173). Next to the park is Fiesta Island, popular for jet skiing and "over the line" baseball.

🕐 Daily 🖐 Free

ℹ 2688 E Mission Bay Drive ☎ 619/276-8200

Museum of Man

The San Diego Museum of Man, located below the California Tower (► 36), offers eclectic, ever-changing exhibits from Californians and Hopi tribes, ancient Egypt and mummies, to the Maya and early man.

✉ 1350 El Prado Drive ☎ 619/239-2001 🕐 Daily 10–4:30 🖐 Inexpensive

Old Town San Diego State Historic Park

The remains of the first European settlement in California, Old Town is preserved with National Park status. The most important area is the Mission San Diego de Alcala, California's first mission, founded in 1769 by Father Junípero Serra. Restored and still used for services, it has beautiful gardens and adobe structures and houses the Museum de Luis Jayme. One of the oldest buildings, Casa de Estudillo, has survived several hundred years.

Old Town Plaza was a general meeting place and center for festivals, religious celebrations and even bullfights in the mid-1800s. Here you'll find the visitors' center, where you can sign up for free tours of the grounds.

✉ San Diego Avenue, at Twiggs Street ☎ 619/220-5422 🕐 Daily 10–5, closed Jan 1, Thanksgiving, Christmas Day 🖐 Free

Presidio Park

Formerly the fort here protected Mission San Diego de Alcala. The park is up the hill from the center of Old Town. As you sit on the benches scattered among the trees of this 50-acre (20ha) park you will have wonderful views of the Old Town expanse. San Diego's landmark museum, the Junipero Serra, sits high atop the hill where California's first mission and presidio were founded. Spanish, Mexican and Native American aspects of San Diego's history are recalled with exhibits of furniture, clothing, household items and other artifacts of the past 200 years.

✉ 2727 Presidio Drive ☎ 619/297-3258 🕐 Park daily; Junipero Serra Museum daily 10–4:30 🖐 Inexpensive

a walk around San Diego

Starting at the Old Town visitors' center, you pass historic buildings, museums and sites that encompass the oldest and most beautiful part of San Diego.

From the visitors' center, walk southward and turn east on San Diego Avenue, continuing to the Machado-Silvas Adobe house.

This is one of the more famous buildings built in the mid-19th century, and houses the Courthouse and the Colorado House/Wells Fargo Museum.

After touring the house, continue a short distance north to Mason Street.

Here you will see the Mason Street School. Built in 1865, this one-room building was San Diego's first publicly owned school.

Go north on Mason to San Diego Avenue, then turn east to Dodson's Corner.

Dodson's Corner is a group of false-front shops where merchants sometimes dress in period costume. Across San Diego Avenue is the San Diego Union Museum, home of the state's longest running newspaper.

From here go north on Twiggs Street to Calhoun Street.

At Calhoun you will see the Steely Stables, and Blackhawk Smith and Stable, both worth a look.

Walk west on Calhoun to the Alvarado House and Johnson House, two beautiful and historic structures. Retrace your steps back to Mason Street, then head south to visit the Casa De Estudillo. After touring the Casa, step across the street back into Old Town Plaza to end your tour.

To complement your stroll through Old Town, you could visit the nearby Gaslamp Quarter, bound by Broadway, 4th, 6th and Harbor streets, which gives a comprehensive history of San Diego's architecture.

Distance 3.5 miles (5.5km)
Time 3 hours
Start point Visitors' Center, Old Town State Historic Park
End point Old Town Plaza
Lunch Old Town Mexican Cafe ($)
✉ 2489 San Diego Avenue
☎ 619/297-4330 🕓 Breakfast, lunch, dinner

San Diego Wild Animal Park

The park, 30 miles (48km) northeast of San Diego, is known for its authentic re-creation of African and Asian terrain. Almost 2,500 endangered animals are presented here by the Zoological Society of San Diego. This 2,100-acre (850ha) preserve features monorail tour, Nairobi Village animal shows, hiking trails and botanical exhibits.

www.wildanimalpark.org

✉ Via Rancho Pkwy exit off I–15 ☎ 619/234-6541 🕐 Daily 9–4

✋ Expensive (combination pass with San Diego Zoo)

Scripps Oceanography and Birch Aquarium

Part of the University of California at San Diego, Birch Aquarium and the Memorial Pier are landmarks of the La Jolla coast. Marine scientists have been working here since the turn of the century. The Institute displays the aquatic world in indoor tanks, an on-shore tidepool and through additional oceanographic exhibits showing the latest advances in oceanography.

✉ 2300 Expedition Way ☎ 858/534-3474 🕓 Daily 9–5 ✋ Moderate

SeaWorld

Perhaps one of, if not *the* finest marine biology park in the world, SeaWorld is impressive, and you can and should plan on spending the better part of a day here. Comfortably spread out over 150 acres (61ha), it features continuous killer whale and dolphin shows, and highly informative marine life exhibits. Between shows, you can touch or view live animals in the petting pools. Also not to miss are the nautical theme playground, marina and state-of-the-art research laboratories.

SeaWorld is home to killer whales Shamu and Baby Shamu, the real stars of the park, as well as seals, sea lions and walruses. The Rocky Point Preserve is a habitat for dolphins and sea otters, while "Penguin Encounter" has over 300 penguins. Other exhibits include "Pets Rule!" and "Fools with Tools." A family-oriented theme park features interactive games and adventures. Guided tours are available, and in the summer there are evening aquatic shows. Owing to the park's popularity, you can expect long waits for some shows and exhibits, especially during the summer. Don't forget the re-entry stamp should you decide to leave the park and return later. Ticket sales stop 90 minutes before closing, which is around sunset most of the year, but up until 11pm in the summer.

www.seaworld.com; **www.**4adventure.com

✉ SeaWorld Drive off the I–5, Mission Bay Park ☎ 619/226-3901 🕓 Daily from 10am, closing times vary with season ✋ Expensive

a walk in Sequoia National Park

This walk takes you through the forest of Sequoia National Park. Even if you visit during the heat of the summer, you will find the temperatures comfortably cool because of the towering foliage.

Begin at the General Sherman Tree, 2 miles (3.2km) east of Giant Forest Village.

The General Sherman tree (named for the Civil War general) is 275ft (84m) high. It is estimated to be more than 2,500 years old and contains enough wood to build 40 houses.

Walk down the self-guided, paved Congress Trail. Cross Sherman Creek on the quaint wooden bridge.

Experience the awesome giant sequoias, like the character-laden Leaning Tree and some lightning-struck and fire-scarred trees as well.

About a mile (1.6km) further, you will meet the junction with the Alta Trail and a grove known as The Senate. A little further along the fern-filled trail is The House Grove.

These two stands are named after the two governing
bodies of the United States government. The path also
visits the McKinley Tree (named for the US president). After
World War II, the practice of naming big trees after politicos
was abandoned.

*Continue a half-mile (0.8km) back, and return to the trail
head. For a longer hike (about six miles/10km), follow the
Congress Trail to the junction of The Trail of the Sequoias.
Take this path for a half-mile (0.8km) to the hike's high
point, then gradually descend one and a half miles
(2.5km) into Long Meadow.*

Lunch before, or after, your hike at Giant Forest Village.

Distance 5 miles (8km)
Time 2–4 hours
Start point General Sherman Tree
End point General Sherman or Long Meadow
unch Grant Grove Restaurant ($$) ✉ Grant Grove Visitors Centre
☎ 559/335-5500, ext 306

SANTA ANA

A typical thriving small city in Orange County, Santa Ana centers around the South Coast Plaza, a European-styled mall with shops, restaurants and cinemas. The **Bowers Museum of Cultural Art,** a mission-style museum, is the largest in Orange County. It focuses on American, Pacific and African art, with an impressive permanent collection and quarterly visiting exhibits.

✚ 10X

Bowers Museum of Cultural Art

✉ 2002 N Main Street ☎ 714/567-3600 🕐 Tue–Sun 10–4 🖐 Inexpensive

SIMI VALLEY

The main reason for visiting Simi Valley is to see the **Ronald Reagan Presidential Library,** set in a beautiful, Spanish mission-style, hilltop mansion. Among the exhibits are photographs and memorabilia of the former US president's life, a full-scale replica of the Oval Office and a large portion of the Berlin Wall.

✚ 9W

Ronald Reagan Presidential Library

✉ 40 Presidential Drive ☎ 800/410-8354 🕐 Daily 10–5; closed major holidays 🖐 Inexpensive

SOLEDAD

Soledad, the oldest settlement in the Salinas Valley, was established in 1791 with the founding of **Mission Nuestra Señora de la Soledad,** 3 miles (5km) west on US 101. The ruins of this adobe mission, along with a restored chapel and museum, can be seen to the east of town.

✚ 5K

Mission Nuestra Senora de la Soledad

✉ Fort Romie Road ☎ 831/678-2586 🕐 Daily 10–4 🖐 Donations

HOTELS

BIG BEAR LAKE
▽▽▽ Apples Bed & Breakfast Inn ($$)
A secluded setting close to shops and recreation.

✉ 42439 Moonridge Road ☎ 909/866-0903;
www.applesbedandbreakfast.com

CATALINA ISLAND
▽▽▽ Hotel Metropole ($$$)
Magnificent ocean views from the rooftop sun deck and spa.

✉ 205 Crescent Avenue, Avalon ☎ 310/510-1884; www.hotel-metropole.com

▽▽▽ Hotel Vista Del Mar ($$)
Resort hotel overlooking beach with larger, comfortable rooms; most with spectacular views.

✉ 417 Crescent Avenue, Avalon ☎ 310/510-1452; www.hotel-vistadelmar.com

DEATH VALLEY
▽▽▽ ▽▽▽ Furnace Creek Inn ($$$)
Native American décor, built in the 1920s. Choose between regular motel-style rooms and furnished cabins.

✉ Call or visit website for directions ☎ 760/786-2345;
www.furnacecreekresort.com ◷ Oct–May only

LAKE ARROWHEAD
Lake Arrowhead Resort ($$)
On the lake in Arrowhead Village. All rooms face the lakefront. Fishing, boating, children's activities.

✉ 27984 Highway 189 ☎ 909/336-1511; www.laresort.com

ORANGE COUNTY
▽▽▽ ▽▽▽ Hilton Waterfront Beach Resort ($$$)
Large resort with beach access, watersports, dining and shopping. All rooms with ocean views.

✉ 21100 Pacific Coast Highway, Huntington Beach ☎ 714/845-8000

♦♦ Hotel Laguna ($$)

A hotel with a history. Affordable and funky, with private beach for guests

✉ 425 S Coast Highway, Laguna Beach ☎ 949/494-1151; www.hotellaguna.com

♦♦♦♦ The Island Hotel Newport Beach ($$$)

One of the finest hotels in the state. Contemporary design with tree-lined swimming pool and tennis courts.

✉ 690 Newport Center Drive, Newport Beach ☎ 949/759-0808; www.theislandhotel.com

PALM SPRINGS

♦♦ The Inn at Deep Canyon ($–$$)

Basic accommodations in Palm Desert; some rooms have kitchenettes.

✉ 74–470 Abronia Trail ☎ 760/346-8061; www.inn-adc.com

♦♦♦♦ Marriott's Desert Springs Resort and Spa ($$$)

Marriott's landmark hotel features an atrium lobby, landscaped gardens, Bob Hope Cultural Center, golf, tennis, man-made beach, an exclusive mall and canopied lagoon boats.

✉ 74855 Country Club Drive, Palm Desert ☎ 760/341-2211; www.desertspringsresort.com

Two Bunch Palms Inn ($$$)

Secluded cottages on 300 acres (120ha). Natural hot springs, a lake and wooded walking paths.

✉ 67425 Two Bunch Palms Trail, Desert Hot Springs ☎ 760/329-8791; www.twobunchpalms.com

SAN DIEGO

♦♦♦ Bay Club Hotel ($$$)

Large rooms, some with private balconies and patios. Situated on the Marina.

✉ 2131 Shelter Island Drive ☎ 619/224-8888; www.bayclubhotel.com

♦♦ Comfort Inn Gaslamp ($$)

In the historic Gaslamp Quarter, and close to the zoo and Balboa Park.

✉ 660 G Street ☎ 619/238-4100; www.comfortinngaslamp.com

♦♦♦ Coronado Island Marriott Resort ($$$)

French and Californian decor on 16 acres (6ha) of exotically landscaped grounds.

✉ 2000 Second Street ☎ 619/435-3000

♦♦♦ Hilton San Diego ($$)

This hotel offers affordable rates near the airport.

✉ 1960 Harbor Island Drive ☎ 619/291-6700

♦♦♦ Horton Grand ($$$)

The oldest building in San Diego (1886). The Horton Grand has Victorian décor with an impressive lobby.

✉ 311 Island Avenue ☎ 619/544-1886; www.hortongrand.com

♦♦♦♦ Hotel del Coronado ($$$)

Famous Victorian hotel from 1880s, jutting out into the bay. Large rooms, some suites. One room is "haunted."

✉ 1500 Orange Avenue ☎ 619/435-6611; www.hoteldel.com

♦♦♦ Humphrey's Half Moon Inn & Suites ($$)

Beautiful gardens and island décor overlooking the bay.

✉ 2303 Shelter Island Drive ☎ 619/224-3411; www.halfmooninn.com

La Costa Resort and Spa ($$$)

Large, luxury resort with golf, tennis and watersports.

✉ 2100 Costa Del Mar Road, Carlsbad ☎ 760/438-9111; www.lacosta.com

♦♦♦♦ The Lodge at Torrey Pines ($$$)

Luxurious five-star accomodations in La Jolla. Overlooks the ocean, craftsman-style architecture.

✉ 11480 North Torrey Pines Road ☎ 858/453-4420;
www.lodgetorreypines.com

RESTAURANTS

ORANGE COUNTY

▼▼▼ Antonello Risorante ($$)
A local favorite serving Northern Italian fare in an elegant setting.
✉ 3800 Plaza Drive, Santa Ana ☎ 714/751-7153 ◷ Lunch Mon–Fri, dinner Mon–Sat

Aubergine ($$$)
Classic French cuisine on the Balboa peninsula. Elegant atmosphere.
✉ 508 29th Street, Newport Beach ☎ 949/723-4150 ◷ Dinner only; closed Mon

▼▼▼ Bistango ($$)
Combination of restaurant and art gallery, offering varied Continental cuisine, prix fixe. Extensive wine list and nightly entertainment.
✉ 19100 Von Karman Avenue, Irvine ☎ 949/752-5222 ◷ Lunch Mon–Fri, dinner daily

Cafe Zoolu ($$)
Funky and eclectic. Known for its vegetarian delights and grilled specialties.
✉ 860 Glenneyre Street, Laguna Beach ☎ 949/494-6825 ◷ Dinner only; closed Mon

Clay Oven ($)
Delightful Indian restaurant with friendly service and great prices. Good lunch buffet.
✉ 15435 Jeffrey Road (Irvine Center), Irvine ☎ 949/552-2851 ◷ Lunch, dinner

Jack Shrimp ($$)
Spicy Cajun, casual environment; moderately priced.
✉ 2400 W Coast Highway, Newport Beach ☎ 949/650-5577 ◷ Lunch (Fri only), dinner

✦✦ Javier's ($$)

Ocean views and large portions. Try the house specialty.

✉ 480 S Coast Highway ☎ 949/474-1239 🕐 Lunch, dinner

McCharles House and Tearoom ($$)

Superb Continental menu. Famous for its desserts. Unique Victorian décor, pleasant patio under huge eucalyptus trees.

✉ 335 S "C" Street, Tustin ☎ 714/731-4063 🕐 Call for opening times

✦✦✦ Oysters ($$)

New and trendy place for fresh seafood and wine from the owner's vineyard. Live entertainment.

✉ 2515 E Coast Highway, Corona del Mar ☎ 949/675-7411 🕐 Dinner only

Stix ($$)

A budget Chinese restaurant offering fast but friendly service.

✉ 28251 Crown Valley Parkway, Laguna Niguel ☎ 949/831-7849 🕐 Lunch, dinner

Tangata ($$)

Continental and South-western cuisine in the Bowers Museum.

✉ 2002 N Main Street, Santa Ana ☎ 714/550-0906 🕐 Lunch only Tue–Sun

✦✦✦ 21 Oceanfront ($$$)

A charming seafood restaurant at the foot of Newport Pier.

✉ 2100 W Oceanfront, Newport Beach ☎ 949/673-2100 🕐 Dinner only

Zinc Café and Market ($)

Stereotypical California, vegetarian coffee-house. Great muffins. Hangout of the arty set. Usually crowded, but worth the wait.

✉ 350 Ocean Avenue, Laguna Beach ☎ 949/494-6302 🕐 Breakfast, lunch only

✦✦✦ Zov's Bistro ($$)

Trendy spot with imaginative Mediterranean cuisine and fresh bread from the on-site bakery.

✉ 17740 E 17th Street, Tustin ☎ 714/838-8855 🕐 Lunch, dinner

PALM SPRINGS/PALM DESERT

✿✿ Las Casuelas Terraza ($)
Mexican food and fantastic margaritas in a relaxing but lively atmosphere.

✉ 222 South Palm Canyon Drive, Palm Springs ☎ 760/325-2794 🕑 Lunch, dinner daily

✿✿✿ Cedar Creek Inn ($$)
Home-town favorite for reliable American food.

✉ 1555 S Palm Canyon Drive ☎ 760/325-7300

✿✿✿ Cuistot ($$$)
A popular and elegant restaurant featuring California-French cuisine. The specialties are veal and rack of lamb. Pricey but worth it.

✉ 72595 El Paseo, Palm Desert ☎ 760/340-1000 🕑 Lunch, dinner; closed Mon

✿✿✿ Palm Springs Chop House ($$$)
Steaks, chops and large side orders, plus tasty desserts.

✉ 262 S Palm Canyon Drive ☎ 760/320-4500 🕑 Dinner only

✿✿✿ Ristorante Mamma Gina ($$)
Authentic northern Italian with homemade pasta, chicken and veal specialties.

✉ 73–705 El Paseo Drive ☎ 760/568-9898 🕑 Lunch, dinner

SAN DIEGO

✿ Anthony's Fish Grotto ($$$)
Family-owned seafood restaurant. Great service, beautiful harbor views. Jacket required.

✉ 1360 Harbor Drive ☎ 619/232-5103 🕑 Lunch, dinner

Athens Market ($$)
No-frills Greek restaurant. Belly dancers on weekends.

✉ 109 W F Street ☎ 619/234-1955 🕑 Lunch Mon–Fri, dinner daily

Cafe Lulu ($)

Coffeehouse/restaurant in the Gaslamp Quarter neighborhood. One of the few late-night places to eat.

✉ 419 F Street ☎ 619/238-0114 🕐 Breakfast, lunch, dinner; no credit cards

▼▼▼ Café Pacifica ($$)

Good seafood specialties in unique, old cemetery setting.

✉ 2414 San Diego Avenue, Old Town ☎ 619/291-6666 🕐 Dinner only

◆ City Delicatessen ($)

Centrally located Jewish deli.

✉ 535 University Avenue ☎ 619/295-2747 🕐 Breakfast, lunch, dinner, open late

Dakota ($)

Mesquite-grilled fish and fowl at good prices. Live music.

✉ 901 5th Avenue ☎ 619/234-5554 🕐 Lunch Mon–Fri, dinner daily

Dick's Last Resort ($)

Continental dining in a converted warehouse.

✉ 345 Fourth Avenue ☎ 619/231-9100 🕐 Lunch, dinner

Le Fontainebleau ($$$)

Expensive French restaurant in The Westgate Hotel. Offers gallery of original oil paintings and award-winning seafood and veal. Pianist.

✉ 1055 Second Avenue ☎ 619/557-3655 🕐 Lunch, dinner

▼▼ Hob Nob Hill ($$)

Family-owned and open since World War II. Specialties include fried scallops and rack of lamb. Kids' menu. Great for breakfast.

✉ 2271 First Avenue (near Balboa Park) ☎ 619/239-8176 🕐 Lunch, dinner

Kansas City Barbeque ($)

No-frills barbecue stand with lots of personality.

✉ 610 W Market Street ☎ 619/231-9680 🕐 Lunch, dinner

▼▼▼ Rainwater's ($$$)

Private club atmosphere with standard American cuisine. Dress code enforced.

✉ 1202 Kettner Boulevard ☎ 619/233-5757 🕐 Lunch, dinner; no lunch on weekends

Thee Bungalow ($$)

This family-run French spot has been pleasing restaurant loyalists for over 30 years.

✉ 4996 West Point Loma Boulevard ☎ 619/224-2884 🕐 Dinner daily

▼▼▼ Umi Sushi ($$)

Traditional sushi offerings, plus tempura, teriyaki and specials.

✉ 2806 Shelter Island Drive ☎ 619/226-1135 🕐 Lunch Mon–Sat, dinner daily

SHOPPING

ART AND ANTIQUES
Antique Row

More than 20 dealers give this street its name.

✉ Adams Avenue, Kensington, San Diego

The Olde Cracker Factory

Antiques center of the area.

✉ 448 W Market, San Diego ☎ 619/233-1669

FASHION
The Paladion

Posh center with Cartier, Tiffany's, Gucci and more.

✉ Across from Horton Plaza, San Diego

ENTERTAINMENT

CONCERT HALLS
Civic Theatre

Ultramodern design provides a great backdrop to concerts held here.

✉ San Diego Concourse, 202 "C" Street, San Diego ☎ 619/615-4100

NIGHTLIFE
Top O' the Cove
Piano bar/restaurant featuring show tunes and standards.
✉ 1216 Prospect Street, La Jolla ☎ 858/454-7779

PERFORMING ARTS/THEATERS
Lawrence Welk Resort Theatre
Dinner theater, with Broadway and Broadway-style shows. Buffet matinee and evening.
✉ 8860 Lawrence Welk Drive, Escondido ☎ 760/749-3448

Orange County Performing Arts Center
Regular performances by New York City Opera, American Ballet Theater and Los Angeles Philharmonic Orchestra, plus presentations of popular musicals.
✉ 600 Town Center Drive, Costa Mesa ☎ 714/556-2787

Sledgehammer Theatre
Avant-garde productions.
✉ 1620 Sixth Avenue, San Diego ☎ 619/544-1484

SPORTS

Eldorado Polo Club
The "Winter Polo Capital of the West." Weekday practice matches are free. Picnic grounds.
✉ 50–950 Madison Street, Indio ☎ 760/342-2223

Mission Hills Resort Golf Club
One reason Palm Springs is "Winter Golf Capital of the World".
✉ 71–501 Dinah Shore Drive, Rancho Mirage, Palm Springs ☎ 760/328-3198

Palm Springs Tennis Center
Nine lit courts open to the public.
✉ 1300 Baristo Road, Palm Springs ☎ 760/320-0020

Index

Acknowledgements

The Automobile Association wishes to thank the following photographers, companies and picture libraries for their assistance in the preparation of this book.

Abbreviations for the picture credits are as follows – (t) top; (b) bottom; (l) left; (r) right; (c) centre; (AA) AA World Travel Library.

4l Hollywood Sign, AA/C Sawyer; **4c** I-5 Freeway, or San Diego Freeway, AA/M Jordan; **4r** Monterey Bay, AA/R Ireland; **5l** Gaslamp Quarter, San Diego, AA/M Jourdan; **5c** Russian Hill, San Francisco, AA/K Paterson; **6/7** Hollywood Sign, AA/C Sawyer; **8/9** Vernal Fall, Yosemite, National Park, AA/R Ireland; **10//11t** Skaters at Venice Beach, AA/C Sawyer; **10ct** Redwoods State Park, Santa Cruz Mountain, AA/K Paterson; **10cb** Sterling Wineries, San Francisco, AA/K Paterson; **10bl** Joshua Tree National Monument Park, Imagestate; **10br** Cascade Lake, Lake Tahoe, AA/R Ireland; **11c** Otani's Hotel Garden in the Sky, Little Tokyo, Los Angeles, AA/M Jourdan; **11b** Beverly Hills Hotel, Sunset Boulevard, Los Angeles, AA/C Sawyer; **12/13t** Grand Central Marks, Los Angeles, AA/M Jourdan; **12bl** Fredericks of Hollywood, Hollywood Boulevard, AA/M Jourdan; **12br** Mel's Diner, AA/M Jourdan; **13t** Fisherman's Wharf, San Franciscon. AA/B Smith; **13b** Couple at outdoors restaurant, Wine Country, AA/H Harris; **14t** Farmer's Market, Los Angeles, AA/C Sawyer; **14/15** Sterling Vineyards, Napa Valley, AA/K Paterson; **15t** Grand Central Market, Los Angeles, AA/C Sawyer; **15c** Mel's Diner, AA/M Jourdan; **15b** Yabu's restaurant, Little Tokyo, Los Angeles, AA/M Jourdan; **16/17** Getty Center, South Promontory, Los Angeles, AA/M Jourdan; **16** Mariposa Grove, Yosemite National Park, AA/R Ireland; **17c** Ride at Knotts Berry Farm, Courtesy of AOCVCB/Knotts Berry Farm; **17bl** Commuters on evening ferry to Sausalito, with Golden Gate Bridge, San Francisco, AA/K Paterson; **17br** Billboard, Sunset Boulevard, AA/C Sawyer; **18/19t** Vineyard, St Helena, Napa Valley, AA/H Harris; **18/19b** Huntington Beach, surfer, AA/C Sawyer; **19** Woman walking along the Walk of Fame, Hollywood, Los Angeles, AA/M Jourdan; **20/21** I-5 Freeway, or San Diego Freeway, AA/M Jordan; **22** In-line skater, Venice Beach, AA/C Sawyer; **24/25** Memorial Day Parade, San Diego, AA/M Jourdan; **26/27** Portal Railway Museum, AA/R Ireland; **28** View of Tour Thru Tree, AA/R Ireland; **29** Policeman, AA/C Sawyer; **34/35** Monterey Bay, AA/R Ireland; **36/37** California Building in Copley Park. Balboa Park; Balboa Park after dark, Balboa Park; **38** Catalina Island, Courtesy of Anaheim/Orange Country Visitor and Convention Bureau; **40** Disneyland® Park, © 2007 Disney Enterprises, Inc; **42** Golden Gate Bridge, San Francisco, AA/K Paterson; **43** Golden Gate Bridge from estuary, AA/K Paterson; **44/45** Hearst Castle from the air, Hearst Castle; **45** Hearst Castle, main library, Hearst Castle; **46** Hollywood Walk of Fame, Los Angeles, AA/C Sawyer; **47** Hollywood Sign, AA/P Wilson; **48** Monterey Bay Aquarium, AA/R Ireland; **48/49** Monterey Bay, AA/R Ireland; **50/51** Yosemite Valley from Tunnel View, Yosemite National Park, AA/R Ireland; **51** Villa Sattiu winery, Napa Valley; AA/H Harris; **52** Big Basin Redwoods State Park, AA/K Paterson; **52/53** Redwood Tree, Redwoods State Park, AA/K Paterson; **54** Yosemite Falls, Yosemite National Park, AA/R Ireland; **54/55** El Capitan Cathedral Rocks, Yosemite National Park, AA/R Ireland; **56/57** Gaslamp Quarter, San Diego, AA/M Jourdan; **58/59** Oceanfront Walk, Venice Beach, Los Angeles, AA/P Wilson; **60** Annual Snow Festival, Snow Festival/North Lake Tahoe, **61** Monarch butterfly, AA/S Day; **62/63** Shopping on Rodeo Drive, Beverly Hills, AA/C Sawyer; **64** Golden Gate Bridge, AA/K Paterson; **66/67** Manhatten Beach, Los Angeles, AA/C Sawyer; **69** Fairground, Santa Monica, AA/P Wilson; **70** Rollerblading in Santa Monica, AA/M Jourdan; **71** Lincoln Golf Course, San Francisco, AA/K Paterson; **72** Exterior of Getty Center, AA/M Jourdan; **73t** Venice Beach, Canal, Los Angeles, AA/M Jourdan; **73b** Malibu number plate, AA/C Sawyer; **74/75** Russian Hill, San Francisco, AA/K Paterson; **77** San Francisco Museum of Modern Art, AA/K Paterson; **78t** Cell in Alcatraz, AA/H Harris; **78b** Ferry in San Francisco Bay, AA/K Paterson; **79** Asian Art Museum, AA/K Paterson; **80/81** Cable Car Museum, AA/K Paterson; **81** Palace of the Legion of Honor, San Francisco, AA/K Paterson; **82/83** Pier 39, Fisherman's Wharf, San Francisco, AA/K Paterson; **84** Chinatown Gate, San Francisco. AA/K Paterson; **85** Lantern, Chinatown, San Francisco, AA/K Paterson; **86** Grace Episcopal Cathedral, San Francisco, AA/K Paterson; **86/87** Hyde Street Pier, San Francisco, AA/K Paterson; **87** Lombard Street, San Francisco, AA/B Smith; **88/89** Mission Dolores, San Francisco, AA/K Paterson; **89** Palace of Fine Arts, AA/K Paterson; **90** Museum of Modern Art, San Francisco, AA/K Paterson; **90/91** Transamerica Pyramid, AA/K Paterson; **91** Wells Fargo History Museum, AA/K Paterson; **99** Pine Ridge Winery, AA/H Harris; **100/101** Winter in Sequoia National Park, Brand X Pictures; **103** Wells Fargo History Museum, AA/K Paterson; **104** Lake Tahoe, AA/R Ireland; **104/105** Lassen Volcanic Park, AA/R Ireland; **106/107** Shasta National Forest, AA/R Ireland; **108/109t** Treasure Island Marina, San Francisco, AA/B Smith; **108/109b** Treasure Island, AA/K Paterson; **110/111** Sacramento Street, San Francisco, AA/K Paterson; **111** Rosicrucian Egyptian Museum, San Jose, AA/K Paterson; **112/113** Rosicrucian Egyptian Museum, San Jose, AA/K Paterson; **113** Winery, St Helena, Napa Valley, AA/K Paterson; **114/115** Pine Ridge Winery, Napa Valley, AA/H Harris; **121** Santa Barbara, AA/C Sawyer; **122/123** Carmel Beach at Sunset, AA/R Ireland; **124** Paseo Neuvo Center, Santa Barbara, AA/C Sawyer; **125** Santa Barbara, AA/C Sawyer; **126/127** Solvang, Alamy, © David Muscroft; **131** Chinatown, Los Angeles, AA/M Jourdan; **132** Sunset Boulevard Sign, Los Angeles, AA/M Jourdan; **132/133** Beverly Hills, Los Angeles, AA/M Jourdan; **133** City Hall, Old Pasadena, Los Angeles, AA/P Wilson; **134t** Beverly Hills Hotel, AA; **134b** Vermont and Sunset Metro Stations, Los Angeles, AA/M Jourdan; **135** Shopping, Rodeo Drive, AA/C Sawyer; **136** Natural History Museum, Los Angeles, AA/M Jourdan; **137t** Stan Laurel Memorial Stone, Los Angeles, AA/P Wilson; **136/137** Central Garden, Getty Center, AA/M Jourdan; **138** Statue of James Dean, Los Angeles, AA/M Jourdan; **138/139t** Huntington Library, Los Angeles, AA/P Wilson; **138/139b** Little Tokyo, Los Angeles, AA/M Jourdan; **140** Long Beach Shoreline Village, Los Angeles, AA/M Jourdan; **1410** Mann's Chinese Theatre, Los Angeles, AA/M Jourdan; **142/143** Venice Beach, Los Angeles, AA/M Jourdan; **153** Death Valley National Monument, Imagestate; **154t** Angel Stadium, Anaheim, Courtesy of AOCVCB/Lovero Group; **154/155** Anaheim Ducks Sculpture, Honda Center, Anaheim, Courtesy of Anaheim/Orange Country Visitor and Convention Bureau; **156/157t** Death Valley National Monument, Brand X Pictures; **156/157b** Joshua Tree National Park, Imagestate; **158/159** Orange County Sunset, Courtesy of Anaheim/Orange County Visitor and Convention Bureau; **160** Snoopy at Knotts Berry Farm, Courtesy of AOCVCB/Knotts Berry Farm; **160/161** Mission San Juan Capistrano, AA/K Paterson; **162** Amtrak Train, Courtesy of Anaheim/Orange County Visitor and Convention Bureau; **162/163** Antique shop in the Olde Towne Orange, Courtesy of AOCVCB/Ellen Clark; **164/165** Surfer, Malibu, AA/M Jourdan; **166/167** International Aerospace Hall of Fame, San Diego, AA/M Jourdan; **168** Star of India, Maritime Museum, San Diego, AA/M Jourdan; **170/171** Gaslamp Quarter, San Diego, AA/M Jourdan; **172/173** San Diego Zoo, Courtesy of Anaheim/Orange County Visitor and Convention Bureau; **174** Sequoia National Park, Brand X Pictures; **175** Sequoia National Park, Brand X Pictures; **176** Discovery Science Center at night, Santa Ana, Courtesy of Anaheim/Orange County Visitor and Convention Bureau

Every effort has been made to trace the copyright holders, and we apologise in advance for any unintentional omissions or errors. We would be pleased to apply any corrections in any following edition of this publication.

Sight locator index

This index relates to the maps on the covers. We have given map references to the main sights in the book. Some sights may not be plotted on the maps.

Dear Reader

Your comments, opinions and recommendations are very important to us. Please help us to improve our travel guides by taking a few minutes to complete this simple questionnaire.

You do not need a stamp (unless posted outside the UK). If you do not want to cut this page from your guide, then photocopy it or write your answers on a plain sheet of paper.

Send to: **The Editor, AA World Travel Guides, FREEPOST SCE 4598, Basingstoke RG21 4GY.**

Your recommendations...

We always encourage readers' recommendations for restaurants, nightlife or shopping – if your recommendation is used in the next edition of the guide, we will send you a **FREE AA Guide** of your choice from this series. Please state below the establishment name, location and your reasons for recommending it.

_____
_____
_____
_____
_____

Please send me **AA Guide** _____

About this guide...

Which title did you buy?

AA _____

Where did you buy it?_____

When? <u>m m</u> / <u>y y</u>

Why did you choose this guide? _____
_____
_____
_____
_____

Did this guide meet your expectations?

Exceeded ☐   Met all ☐   Met most ☐   Fell below ☐

Were there any aspects of this guide that you particularly liked? _____
_____
_____
_____

continued on next page...

Is there anything we could have done better? _____
_____
_____
_____

About you...
Name (*Mr/Mrs/Ms*) _____
Address _____
_____ Postcode _____

Daytime tel nos _____
Email _____

Please only give us your mobile phone number or email if you wish to hear from us about
other products and services from the AA and partners by text or mms, or email.

Which age group are you in?
Under 25 ☐   25–34 ☐   35–44 ☐   45–54 ☐   55–64 ☐   65+ ☐

How many trips do you make a year?
Less than one ☐   One ☐   Two ☐   Three or more ☐

Are you an AA member? Yes ☐   No ☐

About your trip...
When did you book? m m / y y   When did you travel? m m / y y

How long did you stay? _____

Was it for business or leisure? _____

Did you buy any other travel guides for your trip? _____

If yes, which ones? _____
_____
_____

Thank you for taking the time to complete this questionnaire. Please send it to us as soon as
possible, and remember, you do not need a stamp (*unless posted outside the UK*).

AA Travel Insurance call 0800 072 4168 or visit www.theAA.com